YOUR NEXT MOVE

The Leader's Guide to Navigating
Major Career Transitions

Michael D. Watkins

Harvard Business Press | Boston, Massachusetts

Library of Congress Cataloging-in-Publication Data

Watkins, Michael, 1956-
    Your next move : the leader's guide to navigating major career transitions /
Michael D. Watkins.
        p. cm.
    ISBN 978-1-4221-4763-4 (hbk. : alk. paper)
    1. Executives. 2. Career development. 3. Promotions. 4. Leadership.
5. Management. I. Title.
    HD38.2.W377 2009
    650.14—dc22

                                                                    2009019392

The paper used in this publication meets the requirements of the American
National Standard for Permanence of Paper for Publications and Documents
in Libraries and Archives Z39.48-1992.

Contents

8. The STARS Portfolio Challenge   179

Leading an organization in which different parts are in different STARS states—start-up, turnaround, accelerated growth, realignment, and sustaining success. Figuring out where to focus and how to build momentum.

Conclusion: Designing Companywide Transition-Acceleration Systems   197

Understanding the critical transitions taking place throughout companies. Building unified transition acceleration systems. Adjusting for types of transitions. Deploying through coaching, programs, and e-learning.

To Shawna

Acknowledgments

This book is dedicated to my wife and business partner, Shawna Slack. Shawna encouraged me to write a sequel to *The First 90 Days* and unflaggingly supported me through the inevitable ups and downs of the writing process. This book truly would never have been written without her.

Many of the examples that are used throughout the book were inspired by conversations I've had with leaders in transition. One outstanding leader in particular, Mark Clouse, offered a wealth of insight into the challenges of making international moves—the chapter on that challenge draws on our many discussions. Other skilled executives whose experiences contributed substantially to this work include Oray Boston, Harald Emberger, Barbara Schwartz, Rick Searer, Doug Soo Hoo, and Bas van Buijtenen. Many thanks to them for sharing their thoughts and recommendations for improving the manuscript.

Some of the survey research discussed in the introduction was done while I visited at IMD, a leading business school located in Lausanne, Switzerland, between September 2007 and June 2008. I also refined some of the ideas through participation in IMD's Orchestrating Winning Performance (OWP) program in June 2008. IMD is a fine business education institution and I feel privileged to have been able to spend time there. Many thanks to the IMD staff there and to wonderful colleagues including Bala

Chakravarthy, Carlos Cordon, Dan Dennsion, Robert Hooijberg, Peter Killing, Don Marchand, Maury Peiperl, Stuart Read, David Robertson, Phil Rosenzweig, Paul Strebel, and Jack Wood. Special thanks to Professor Jean-François Manzoni and to his family for all the encouragement and support they gave us, professionally and personally, during our year in Switzerland.

Finally many thanks to Jeff Kehoe and Roberta Fusaro at Harvard Business Publishing. Jeff has been both a strong advocate for my work for many years and a highly valued adviser. Roberta is one of the most gifted editors with whom I've had the pleasure to work.

Introduction

Your Next Move

YOU'VE GOT BIG IDEAS AND AMBITIONS IN YOUR CAREER, and you've done well . . . so far. But are you ready for your next move? Because your path to the top will be built step-by-step through a series of major career moves. And each time you make a change, you have the opportunity to shine or to stumble. Shine and you will be positioned for still greater things. Stumble and you may never recover.

Dissect the CV of any successful executive, and you'll see a series of high-stakes transitions into ever-more-challenging roles: from individual contributor all the way to general management. Through hard-won experience, the best and brightest get promoted and learn to lead others. They seek out greener pastures (and greater challenges) at new companies or business units—and learn to adapt to unfamiliar cultures. The path to still-greater corporate heights often leads them through international assignments or different functional areas of the business—and likely both. If all goes well, they win responsibility for whole businesses—and all that entails.

This could be your story too. But only if your next move is a successful one. Regardless of whether you've been promoted or are joining a new company or are taking on any of the other classic transitions that executives make in their careers, your next move will be a defining moment. Because every transition is a pivotal time when you either gain traction that propels you forward or dig yourself into a very deep hole.

I've spent the last decade exploring how leaders succeed or fail in making transitions to challenging new roles. My early work, as chronicled in *The First 90 Days*, was about the common principles that leaders can apply in any transition as they strive to build personal credibility, create alliances, and secure early wins in their new roles.

Since that book was published, I've worked with hundreds of leaders who have applied *The First 90 Days* concepts and tools to learn and plan during their transitions. While thankful for the help, they also posed challenging questions—most of which revolved around how to apply the principles in diverse transition situations.

> "I've been promoted from VP of marketing to country manager, and I'm struggling to know what I need to focus on."

> "I've moved from an operating role to a regional HR position and feel like I'm wading in quicksand."

> "I've been transferred to a supply chain role in China and haven't a clue how to operate in the culture."

Your Next Move is my answer to those questions. It flows from a fundamental observation: the way you go about making your next move will vary dramatically depending on the type of move you are making. While the principles from *The First 90 Days* can usefully be applied in every situation, the way you apply them is entirely different when you get promoted to a higher level than when you shift to a different function, or enter a new organizational culture, or move to a new country. If you fail to understand the unique demands of the diverse career transitions you will encounter, you may be setting yourself up for a career-ending fall.

The First 90 Days

I wrote *The First 90 Days* because transitions into new roles are the most challenging times in the lives of business leaders. Think that's an exaggeration? Consider the results of a recent survey I conducted at IMD, the leading European business school: fully 87 percent of the 143 senior HR professionals who responded either agreed or strongly agreed with the statement, "Transitions into significant new roles are the most challenging times in the professional lives of managers." Fully 70 percent agreed or strongly agreed that "success or failure during the transition period is a strong predictor of overall success or failure in the job."[1]

Transitions are leadership crucibles because actions during the first few months have a disproportionate impact on overall success or failure. In successful transitions, leaders establish themselves and build credibility; they find ways to leverage themselves and create virtuous cycles in which success breeds confidence and the political capital to take on ever-larger challenges. In failed transitions, leaders fail to thrive; they create downward spirals and vicious cycles that deplete their energy and demoralize their organizations.

When I started doing research on transitions, far too many managers had to learn the hard way how to make good transitions. They pursued a sink-or-swim process I called "leadership development through Darwinian evolution." This was a terrible waste, because my research showed that there are fundamental imperatives and supporting tools that can be applied to accelerate leadership transitions at all levels. Through study and years of work with executives at leading companies such as Johnson & Johnson, I developed a set of basic principles and supporting tools that can be applied in every transition. The core First 90 Days principles are summarized in the box, "The Seven Elements of Successful Transitions."

The Seven Elements of Successful Transitions

1. *Organize to learn.* Figure out what you most need to learn, from whom, and how you can best learn it. Focus on the right mix of technical, cultural, and political learning.

2. *Establish A-list priorities.* Identify a few vital goals and pursue them relentlessly. Think early about what you need to accomplish by the end of year one in the new position.

3. *Define strategic intent.* Develop and communicate a compelling mission and vision for what the organization will become. Outline a clear strategy for achieving the mission and realizing the vision.

4. *Build the leadership team.* Define your assessment criteria and evaluate the team you inherited. Move deftly to make the necessary changes; find the optimal balance between bringing in outside talent and promoting high-potential leaders within the organization.

5. *Lay the organizational foundation for success.* Identify the most important supporting changes you need to make in the structure, processes, and key talent bases of the organization. Put a plan in place for addressing the most pressing organizational weaknesses.

6. *Secure early wins.* Build personal credibility and energize people by identifying "centers of gravity" where you can get some early successes. Organize the right set of initiatives to secure early wins.

7. *Create supportive alliances.* Identify how the organization really works and who has influence. Understand who needs to champion your success and create key alliances in support of your initiatives.

I published this early thinking about transitions never imagining the impact *The First 90 Days* would have. With sales of around half a million copies in English so far, and translation into twenty-six languages, the book clearly struck a chord, responding to an urgent and ongoing need in people's work lives. The fact that the book continues to sell strongly year after year, through boom times and recessions, shows that transitions are an eternal leadership challenge that every generation confronts anew.

Mapping Common Career Moves

Since *The First 90 Days* was published in 2003, I have watched transition acceleration thinking take root and help hundreds of thousands of leaders enter new roles. But the more work I did with leaders in transition, the more I found myself thinking about their struggles with specific situations. How should the seven elements be applied in diverse transition contexts? It became clear that leaders experienced very different challenges when they were promoted, for example, from when they moved to a new company.

So I decided to catalog the types of transitions leaders experience during their careers and to think about the implications for how they could all be accelerated. Doing so was relatively straightforward, because I'd been surveying participants in my transition acceleration programs for many years on the types of moves they were experiencing. Delving into this data revealed that most leaders experience some or all of the following types of transitions at some point in their professional lives: promotion to a higher level, onboarding into a new company, moving to a new geographic location with an unfamiliar culture, being asked to lead people who were formerly their peers, turning around an organization in trouble, realigning a business that is drifting into trouble, and so on. A group of ninety participants that I taught in a Harvard Business School general management program, for example, averaged sixteen years of business experience. In that time the average participant had experienced 5.5 promotions, worked for 2.4 companies, shifted between business functions 2.7 times, and made 1.5 international moves. Never mind that they had experienced many hidden transitions when they got new bosses, or their responsibilities shifted when they were given additional responsibilities, or the organization itself changed in significant ways while their titles remained the same.

After much thought, I selected eight common types of career moves as representative types; each is the subject of a chapter in this book.

1. *The promotion challenge:* Moving to a higher level in the hierarchy and understanding what "success" looks like at the new level, including issues of focus, delegation, developing leadership competencies, and demonstrating "presence."

2. *The leading-former-peers challenge:* An important variant of promotion in which the leader is elevated to manage a team including his or her former peers, with the associated challenges of establishing authority and altering existing relationships.

3. *The corporate diplomacy challenge:* Moving from a position of authority to one in which effectiveness in influencing others and building alliances is critical for getting things done.

4. *The onboarding challenge:* Joining a new organization and grappling with the need to adapt to a new culture, develop the right political "wiring," and align expectations up, down, and sideways.

5. *The international move challenge:* Leading people in an unfamiliar ethnic culture while at the same time moving one's family and creating a new support system.

6. *The turnaround challenge:* Taking over an organization that is in deep trouble and figuring out how to save it from destruction.

7. *The realignment challenge:* Confronting an organization that is in denial about the need for change and creating a sense of urgency before emerging problems erupt in a crisis.

8. *The business portfolio challenge:* Leading an organization in which different parts are at different STARS states—start-up, turnaround, accelerated growth, realignment, and sustaining success—and figuring out where to focus and how to build momentum

This is by no means a definitive list of all the possible moves business leaders experience during their careers. Absent are moves from one business function to another—for example, from sales to marketing—as well as the challenge of being assigned a cross-functional project role. Also missing are some specific organizational-change challenges such as integrating an acquisition or shutting down a failed operation.

In the end, however, I had to balance the competing demands of completeness and compactness. The eight types are a reasonably comprehensive catalog of the critical moves most business leaders make at some point in their careers. They are nearly universal in today's professional careers; their ubiquity and perpetual nature means leaders who can deal with them effectively will be much more successful overall. In fact, if you can deal with these eight tough transitions, you can deal with virtually anything!

Understanding the Core Challenges

What does it take to be successful in each of these distinct types of career moves? Detailed advice is provided in the chapters that follow. Before getting there, however, it's worth taking a step back and asking, What is it that makes different types of career moves challenging? Are there some overarching guidelines for applying the seven transition elements in these diverse situations? The more I thought about these questions, the clearer it became that every major career move really revolves around two core challenges. I call them the *personal adaptive challenge* and the *organizational-change challenge*.

The Personal Adaptive Challenge

The personal adaptive challenge is what you, the leader, need to work on *in yourself* to be successful in your new role. Given your history, mind-set, and capabilities, what are the most important personal shifts you personally need to make when you get promoted, join a new company, or move internationally? What do you need to do more of and less of? What new competencies do you need to develop? What adjustments in your style do you need to make?

Armed with clarity about your personal adaptive challenge, you can design your plan for managing yourself. This means embracing the key pillars of self-management: enhancing self-awareness, exercising personal discipline, building complementary teams, and leveraging advice-and-counsel networks.

Enhancing self-awareness. It's essential that you understand your reflexive responses to new management challenges: How do you learn in novel situations? How do you prefer to make decisions? Leadership style assessments can help you gain insight, as can 360-degree and other observational feedback. Competency assessments likewise can be very helpful in identifying gaps to be filled.

It's crucial to do this because it's all too easy to end up doing things that may be perceived as "normal" in one environment, but that label you as "dangerous" or "ineffectual" in another. Once a negative opinion begins to crystallize, it creates a vicious cycle in which *expectations* shape perceptions to create self-fulfilling prophecies. Once the die is cast, it is extremely difficult to turn things around; prevention is the key to survival.

Exercising personal discipline. You need to adapt yourself to the demands of the new role and not vice versa. As I put it in *The First 90 Days*, "Your weaknesses can make you vulnerable, but so can your strengths . . . The qualities that have made you successful so far can prove to be weaknesses in your new role."[2] Wise leaders in transition therefore ask themselves, "What am I good at (or enjoy doing) that I need to do less of?" and "What am I not so good at (or don't like doing) that I need to do more of?" And then they consciously, deliberately fight to make those things happen every day.

Building complementary teams. You simply can't do it all, no matter the business context, and you shouldn't try to turn yourself into something or someone you're not. Fortunately, you don't have to lead the business all by yourself; you can build a team to support you. As you build your team, however, it's important to think in terms of creating one that complements you. Beware the lure of selecting a bunch of clones and creating your own personal echo chamber.

Leveraging advice-and-counsel networks. Finally, build an advice-and counsel network that will help you to maintain perspective and exercise sound judgment.[3] Leaders always need a network of people who can provide advice and counsel, but the right mix depends on the role. The implication is that the advice-and-counsel network that served you well in your last role is unlikely to be what you need in your new role. The more senior you become, for example, the more likely it is that you need wise political counselors in your network, both knowledgeable insiders in your organization and impartial outsiders.

Without question, self-awareness is the most important of these four pillars. It's the foundation upon which all your efforts at self-management will be built. Armed with a healthy dose of self-insight you will know what to discipline yourself to do and not to, what kinds of advice and counsel will be most helpful, as well as who your natural complements are likely to be. Without it, you will be stumbling around in the dark.

Each of the chapters that follow begins with a short illustrative case study of a leader in transition. So as you read each one, think about the personal adaptive challenges they are facing. To what extent are they, or should they be, using the tools of self-management to speed their adaptation to their new roles?

The Organizational-Change Challenge

Whereas the personal adaptive challenge is about you, the organizational-change challenge is what you need to accomplish *in the business.* What is the current state of the organization? Who are the key stakeholders? What do they expect you to accomplish and in what time frame? What resources do you have to work with? What will "success" look like and feel like?

Armed with clarity about your organizational challenge, you can design your plan for building momentum in the business by applying the First 90 Days principles. In doing this it helps to have a framework for assessing the state of the business and defining key objectives. I developed the STARS model to help new leaders figure out how to assess the business situation and tailor their strategies accordingly. (The STARS model is discussed in greater detail in chapter 8.)

STARS is an acronym for five common situations leaders may find themselves moving into: *start-up, turnaround, accelerated growth, realignment,* and *sustaining success.*[4] The model outlines the characteristics and challenges of, respectively, launching a venture or project; getting one back on track; dealing with rapid expansion; reenergizing a once-leading company that's now facing serious problems; and following in the footsteps of a highly regarded leader with a strong legacy of success. Have you inherited an organization, product, project, or process that is (1) in the early stages of being launched, (2) in crisis, (3) hitting its stride and growing rapidly, (4) drifting into difficulty, or (5) successful but confronting maturity? The key characteristics of each of these common organizational-change challenges are summarized in figure I-1.

Crystallizing Your Challenges

A thorough understanding of your personal adaptive challenge and organizational-change challenge is the essential foundation for success in any leadership transition. By crystallizing these two

FIGURE I-1

The STARS model

Start-up	Turnaround	Accelerated growth	Realignment	Sustaining success
Assembling the capabilities (people, financing, and technology) to get a new business or initiative off the ground	Saving a business or initiative widely acknowledged to be in serious trouble	Managing a rapidly expanding business	Reenergizing a previously successful organization that now faces problems	Coming in on the heels of a highly regarded leader with a stellar record of accomplishment
Challenges				
Building the strategy, structures, and systems from scratch without a clear framework or boundaries	Reenergizing demoralized employees and other stakeholders	Putting in place structures and systems to permit scaling	Convincing employees that change is necessary	Living in the shadow of the former leader and managing the team he or she created
Recruiting and welding together a high-performing team	Making effective decisions under time pressure	Integrating many new employees	Carefully restructuring the top team and refocusing the organization	Playing good defense before embarking on too many new initiatives
Making do with limited resources	Going deep enough with painful cuts and difficult personnel choices			Finding ways to take the business to the next level
Opportunities				
You can do things right from the beginning.	Everyone recognizes that change is necessary.	The potential for growth helps to motivate people.	The organization has significant pockets of strength.	A strong team may already be in place.
People are energized by the possibilities.	Affected constituencies offer significant external support.	People will be inclined to stretch themselves and those who work for them.	People want to continue to see themselves as successful.	People are motivated to continue their history of success.
There are no rigid preconceptions.	A little success goes a long way.			A foundation for continued success (such as a long product pipeline) may be in place.

core challenges you will be able to develop the right plans for managing yourself and creating momentum in the organization. When I coach executives and work with leaders in transition programs, I really pound away on this, telling them, "If you can get crystal clear in your own mind what these two challenges are, it becomes straightforward to put together plans to meet them."

I've also found that it's very important to commit your understanding of these two core challenges to writing and to revisit them on a regular basis. A crisp statement of your personal adaptive challenge provides you with the insight necessary to manage yourself by, for example, disciplining yourself to do things that don't come naturally. Likewise, a crisp statement of the organizational change provides you with the insight necessary to translate the First 90 Days principles into practice to create momentum in the business.

So if you are currently in transition, take a few minutes to reflect on these challenges. Get out a sheet of paper and complete these statements:

> My personal adaptive challenge (what I need to work on in myself) is:

> My organizational-change challenge (what I need to work on in the organization) is:

Plan for the Book

The book is organized roughly into two parts, starting with an exploration of common personal adaptive challenges and then examining common organizational-change challenges. Each of the chapters begins with a story of a leader in transition. These stories are disguised versions of real situations; the names of the leaders and the companies of which they are a part have been altered.

Chapters 1 through 5 focus, respectively, on the challenges of getting promoted, leading former peers, moving from positions of authority to influence, joining new organizations, and making international moves. Each chapter not only provides detailed advice for meeting the challenge; it also develops a tool that can usefully be applied in a range of other situations. While you'll of course read the chapters that are most immediately applicable to your situation, you will find useful ideas and tools in many of the other chapters. Also, in my experience most leaders experience multiple shifts in parallel—for example, getting promoted and moving to a new location.

In chapter 1, which focuses on the promotion, for instance, I not only explore the challenges that are common to every promotion; I also use a variant of the leadership pipeline model to explore level-specific challenges and provide a still deeper look at the "seismic shifts" leaders experience when they become general managers for the first time.[5]

The second chapter, on leading former peers, introduces the idea of *relationship reengineering*, exploring what it takes to alter existing relationships with people who were formerly peers and now are direct reports. The basic ideas, however, can be applied in any situation in which existing relationships must be transformed after a significant transition has taken place.

Chapter 3, on corporate diplomacy, focuses on how you can move from a position of authority to one in which influence is essential to getting things done. I explore how leaders can map the influence landscape, identify agendas and alignments, and build supportive alliances. The basic influence toolbox, while obviously critical when you make this type of move, can be applied in virtually any transition.

In chapter 4, which focuses on onboarding, I introduce the idea of "organizational immunology," the notion that cultures are the organizational equivalent of the human immune system and that bringing in a new leader is like doing an organ transplant. This leads naturally to a discussion of how new leaders can best avoid being rejected by the culture. It provides tools that can be applied any time your next move involves adapting to a new culture or subculture (for example, moving between units of the same company).

I end the first part of the book with chapter 5, a look at what it takes to make successful international moves. Here the focus is not just on leading in a new ethnic culture, but about establishing new personal support systems for yourself and your family. Although this is most critical when you are making an international move, the ideas can be applied to help minimize the impact on your family of any major career move.

The primary focus in these first five chapters is on personal adaptive challenges. But as you read them, you will encounter leaders who are dealing with a broad array of organizational-change challenges too. In chapter 1, for example, you will be introduced to a leader who has just been promoted to general management for the first time. While he is confronting tough personal adaptive challenges, he is simultaneously wrestling with what it means to sustain the success of a strong business.

Likewise in chapter 4, you will meet a leader who is moving from a sustaining-success environment in one company to an accelerated-growth situation in another. While much of his struggle revolves around adapting to a very different corporate culture, the demands of an unfamiliar business situation are very much a factor.

However, these common types of organizational-change challenges are in the background in the first part of the book. In the final three chapters they move to center stage using the STARS model. Chapter 6 explores the challenges of turning around a business that is in very deep trouble. It provides some powerful tools—business systems analysis and 3-D Business Strategy—that also can be applied in a broad array of other situations.[6]

The focus shifts to the challenge of proactive change in chapter 7. Here the issue is how to create a sense of urgency and build momentum when many in the organization may be in denial about the need for transformation. It also explores how leaders need to adapt their styles to different types of business situations, contrasting heroic leadership with stewardship.

Then in chapter 8, I discuss how leaders can best manage the complexities that arise when they (inevitably) inherit a mix of STARS situations and need to figure out how best to allocate their energies. In addition to providing a tool for mapping STARS portfolios, the chapter gives guidance on how to marshal organizational energy and create "execution engines" in order to secure early wins.

Finally, in the conclusion, I step back from individual transitions and examine the implications of the career moves framework for businesses as a whole. Transitions into new roles go on all the time in most companies.[7] Cumulatively, their success or failure has a major impact on overall organizational performance. Given that independent research has found that the right transition support can yield 30 to 40 percent reductions in time to performance for leaders taking new roles, organizational transition acceleration is an essential element of enterprise risk management and a potential source of competitive advantage.[8] So I look at how companies can best support these leaders, laying out some basic principles for creating transition-acceleration systems.

In summary, this book is about how leaders can survive and thrive in the classic career changes that virtually everyone faces on

Getting Access to Online Resources

While this book stands on its own as a resource for making your next move, additional resources are available online. If you are currently in transition or about to enter a new role, the place to start is with a tool I developed to identify the types of transitions you are experiencing (many leaders experience multiple types at the same time) and identify which chapters and additional online resources are likely to be of greatest interest. To access the tool and other resources, just go to the Web site for the book, www.YourNextMove.net.

their road to the top. The chapters that follow build on my work in *The First 90 Days*, but delve much more deeply into the distinct, tough transitions that leaders face. You will get clear road maps—advice and tools—to surmount the challenges associated with your next move . . . and every one after that.

1 The Promotion Challenge

BERT VANDERVLIET HAD BEEN WORKING STEADILY TOWARD this promotion for years. But just four months into his new job, as a business unit leader at BSC Chemicals, the euphoria was beginning to wear off: the realities of what it would take to lead the company's plastic resins manufacturing unit were becoming evident—and Bert was wondering if he was fully prepared for the challenges of handling a global business with more than three thousand employees worldwide.

Bert had spent his entire fifteen-year career at BSC, a maker of specialty chemicals, plastics, and pharmaceuticals headquartered in Belgium. He had joined BSC's performance plastics unit soon after completing his master's degree. Even in his first job, as an assistant product manager, he had won early recognition for his leadership abilities. Bert's strong performance continued, and eventually he was assigned to help set up the performance plastics unit's new Asian business center in Singapore. He quickly built up the sales side of that venture and was promoted to sales manager. In addition to the sales responsibility, he was also charged with managing the subcontracting of BSC's plastics production, so Bert ended up gaining some good exposure to the manufacturing side of the business.

When he returned to Belgium three years later, he was promoted to European marketing and sales director, overseeing a group of eighty professionals in technical marketing, sales, and customer service. He also became a member of that unit's top management team, which allowed him to experience decision making at the business-unit level and to familiarize himself with what was going on in other functions. In due course, he was transferred to BSC's polyethylene division as a vice president of marketing and sales, responsible for a cluster of products, related services, and a staff of nearly two hundred.

Now recognized as one of the future leaders of the company with twelve years of experience, Bert was asked to join BSC's corporate human resources organization. He was responsible for internal sourcing and external recruitment of executives, a role he held for almost three years. This gave him a deeper understanding of HR, a broader view of the company's operations, a chance to build an organization-wide network, and greater visibility with BSC's senior executives.

All of Bert's hard work culminated in his appointment as the business unit leader for plastic resins, a sister unit of performance plastics in BSC's plastic materials division. The resins business manufactured the raw material for fabricating plastic components. It was relatively small but one of BSC's best-performing units. Quite intentionally, the senior team at BSC had assigned Bert to a successful business with a strong team that could help him learn what it meant to head up a thriving unit and, over time, push his leadership skills to the next level. The setup was perfect, completely in his favor—yet Bert was astonished at how much he was struggling to climb the learning curve.

He fretted about the high expectations placed on him; after all, when you inherit a successful business, there's often no place to go but down. The resins business was highly profitable but mature—which presented Bert with a very different set of challenges than he had experienced in the high-growth performance plastics business. He worried that any significant misstep could seriously limit his future prospects at BSC.

Bert also quickly recognized the difference between leading a particular functional group, as he had in the past, versus overseeing multiple functional areas within a complete business. Most of the people Bert was leading now knew much more about operations, say, or R&D, than he did. Yet they were expecting him to make the right trade-offs between the supply and demand sides of the business (operations versus marketing and sales) and between focusing on current results and investing in the future (finance versus R&D). Because of the cross-functional nature of his new role, *Bert felt much less rooted in any one area of expertise,* and thus much less confident in his ability to discern the strengths and weaknesses of his team.

Bert was also now leading many more employees than he ever had. In his other management roles at BSC, he had been able to initiate a reasonable degree of personal contact, albeit sometimes sporadic, with most of his employees—something that was simply impossible in this new role, with more than three thousand people scattered in facilities around the globe. The implications of this became clear to him as he worked with his team to craft the annual strategy. When the time came to communicate it to the organization, he realized that he couldn't go out and simply sell the vision and strategy by himself; he had to work more through his direct reports and find other channels for spreading the word. And after touring most of the unit's facilities, Bert likewise worried that he'd never really be able to keep in touch with what was happening on the front lines.

As a member of various management teams during his tenure at BSC, Bert had gained some appreciation for how difficult it was for business heads to prioritize all the issues thrown at them in any given day, week, or month. Still, Bert was surprised by the scope and complexity of the problems at this level. He wasn't sure how to allocate his time and immediately felt overloaded. He knew he needed to delegate more, but he wasn't clear yet about which tasks and assignments he could safely leave to others.

Never mind that Bert had also recently become aware of some potentially dangerous patterns in how he was managing his new team in the plastic resins unit. A month earlier, his vice president of HR, an experienced and insightful executive, offered the new leader some blunt but friendly feedback: "You seem to be over-managing your VP of sales and marketing. You need to give Kurt a little space." The HR executive also suggested that Bert be a bit more careful about how and when he raised new ideas in meetings with the senior team. "I know you're just trying to get the group to be more open and flexible, but they worry that they need to mobilize around every brainstorm."

Finally, Bert was still adjusting to the increasing external demands on his time. While he had of course listened in on analyst calls in the past, he was now expected to lead the discussions and field tough questions. Other types of requests were flooding in to the unit leader's support staff, as well: Could Bert participate in important industry/government forums sponsored by the corporate government affairs group? Would Bert be willing to sit for an interview with an editor from *Forbes* magazine? Could Bert speak at the various industry conferences, awards ceremonies, and other events happening locally and overseas within the next few months?

The Promotion Challenge

As Bert's experience suggests, a promotion definitely marks the end of years of hard work to persuade influential people in the organization that you're willing and able to move to the next level. But it also marks the beginning of a new journey in which you must figure out what it takes to excel in the new role, how to exceed the expectations of those who promoted you, and how to position yourself for still-greater things. That's the promotion challenge.

What does it take to meet this challenge? In *The First 90 Days*, I stressed the importance of "promoting yourself." Rest assured, I was not advocating the ego-driven selling of oneself, but rather, highlighting the need for executives to prepare themselves mentally to move to the next level of the organization and to meet any personal-change challenges. As I put it in that book, promoting yourself doesn't mean believing that you will be successful in your new job by continuing to do what you did in your previous job, only more so. It means letting go of the past and embracing the imperatives of the new situation.[1]

As you work to promote yourself, it also helps to *distinguish between challenges that are common to most promotions and challenges that are specific to the level and position to which you're ascending.* The common challenges flow, in large part, from predictable changes in the information-processing demands placed on leaders as they rise up through organizations. As I will discuss in the following sections, for example, coping with increasing issue breadth and complexity requires leaders to *rethink how and what they delegate each time they get promoted.*

But it's not enough to focus on these common promotion challenges, because there are specific, level-dependent competencies that leaders must develop to be successful. It's here that newly promoted leaders tend to get into the most trouble; their experience better prepares them to deal with the common challenges of promotion (e.g., delegating differently) than to develop wholly new level-specific competencies.

Bert Vandervliet, for example, is trying to figure out what it means to move from a functional vice president's role to a true general management job. To solve this riddle, he'll need to identify both the core challenges and competency gaps he faces, and then organize himself to deal with them most effectively. He'll have to exercise personal discipline to do things he normally wouldn't, build a team that complements him, and think hard about what advice and counsel he'll need and how he'll use it.

Core Promotion Challenges

Many of the core promotion challenges leaders face, listed below, are actually by-products of the different information-processing and influence demands transitioning executives encounter at higher levels of the organization.

- Your *impact horizon*, or the range of issues and challenges you have a direct hand in addressing, broadens significantly as you move up; you are juggling more things and are forced to do more multitasking.

- The *complexity and ambiguity* of what you have to deal with increases: for any given issue, there are many more variables to consider, and cause-and-effect relationships often become less clear as you move to higher levels of the organization.

- *Organizational politics* become more challenging at higher levels; peers and bosses are more capable and have stronger personalities.

- You need to lead *farther from the front lines*, which can make it difficult to communicate strategy downward and stay informed about what's happening on the ground.

- You are under *more scrutiny* by more people, more frequently; there are fewer private moments when you are not on stage.

For each of these common core challenges, there are associated strategies for what you need to do to promote yourself. (See figure 1-1.)

FIGURE 1-1

Core promotion challenges

For each core challenge there are corresponding strategies that newly promoted leaders should employ.

What's really changed?	What should you do?
Broader impact horizon: There is a broader range of issues, people, and ideas to focus on.	Balance depth and breadth.
Greater complexity and ambiguity: There are more variables, and there is greater uncertainty about outcomes.	Delegate more deeply.
Tougher organizational politics: There are more powerful stakeholders to contend with.	Influence differently.
Further from the front lines: There is greater distance between you and the people executing on the ground, potentially weakening communication and adding more filters.	Communicate more formally.
More scrutiny: There is more attention paid to your actions by more people, more frequently.	Adjust to greater visibility.

Balance Breadth and Depth

Each time you're promoted, your *impact horizon* broadens to encompass a wider set of issues and decisions. Whereas Bert was formerly focusing on his function and its impact on the larger business, now he has to deal with the full array of issues affecting the unit.

To deal with this increase in scope, leaders have to be able to gain and sustain an integrative view of the business. In *The Nature of Leadership*, authors B. Joseph White and Yaron Prywes describe this as a "helicopter view"—a broad perspective on the organization, encompassing its past, present, and future.[2]

But the leader-as-helicopter metaphor has even richer possibilities: Helicopters don't just hover; they move up or down in response to the pilot's needs. In the context of promotions and transition challenges, it's helpful to remember that even as you gain managerial altitude and perspective, you must preserve your ability to dive deep into issues when the situation demands it. You can't afford to always stay at fifty thousand feet. You have to be able to pick an issue of concern and start digging into it, asking questions and pushing for answers until you are confident there is a firm foundation for people's opinions and judgments. Doing this well means knowing which are the critical "fulcrum issues" that now or will impact the business, which in turn rests on your ability to gain and sustain the integrative view. It also means, as I will discuss shortly, being an effective "problem finder."

You need to do this selectively, of course, and you need to be able to move back up to a higher level once you're satisfied: it's dangerous to hover near ground level for too long, regardless of how interesting the scenery is. This is especially the case if you find yourself focusing too much on the business activities or functions you were involved with before you were promoted. The concerns raised by the VP of HR that Bert was "overmanaging" his VP of sales and marketing suggest that he might be at risk of falling into this trap.

Understanding when to keep soaring and when to swoop down for a closer look is something that every leader needs to relearn each time he or she gets promoted—because the fifty-thousand-foot view in your previous leadership role may just be the world at five thousand feet, or even five hundred feet, in your new job. Key here is to have early discussions with advisors about how to approach this. It also helps to identify one or more role models, people who are viewed as highly effective at the level to which you have been promoted. Talk to them or people who have worked with them if you can; study them from a distance if you can't.

Rethink What You Delegate

The complexity and ambiguity of the issues you are dealing with will increase as you move into a new role—which means you'll need to reorganize your approach to handling particular projects, products, processes, and so on. In particular, you'll need to rethink what you delegate.

Management sage Peter Drucker said it as far back as the early 1950s: the ability to delegate lies at the heart of leadership.[3] Regardless of where you land in the organization, the keys to effective delegation remain pretty much the same: you build a team of competent people whom you trust, you establish goals and metrics through which you can monitor people's progress, you translate higher-level goals into specific responsibilities for your direct reports, and you reinforce them through some sort of management-by-objectives process. In other words, the "how" of delegation is a constant.

However, "what" you delegate—the basic units of analysis through which you engage with your direct reports—often needs to change when you get promoted. If you are leading an organization of five people, it may make sense to delegate specific tasks such as drafting a piece of marketing material or pursuing a particular customer. In an organization of fifty people, your focus may shift from tasks to projects and processes. At five hundred people, you often need to delegate responsibility for specific products or platforms. And at five thousand people, your direct reports may be responsible for whole businesses, and so on.

Influence Differently

Conventional wisdom says that the higher up in the organization you go, the easier it is to get things done. Not necessarily. Paradoxically, when you get promoted, positional authority becomes less rather than more important for pushing agendas forward. You may indeed have increased scope to make decisions that affect the business, but there are significant differences in the ways you need to make those decisions. The process becomes more political—less about authority, and more about influence— which isn't good or bad, simply inevitable.

There are two major reasons why this is so. First, the issues you're dealing with become much more complex and ambiguous when you move up a level—and your ability to identify "right" answers based on data and analysis declines accordingly. In this milieu, decisions are shaped more by others' expert judgments and dominant worldviews, so, despite your positional authority, it's actually the people who exhibit that expertise and create those worldviews who have the most influence on what happens.

Second, at a higher level of the organization, critical constituencies are more capable and have stronger egos. Remember, you were promoted because you are able and driven; the same is true for everyone around you—peers, bosses, and other stakeholders. So it shouldn't come as a complete surprise that the decision-making game becomes that much more bruising and politically charged the higher up you go. It's critical, then, for you to become more effective at building and sustaining alliances and for you to become expert in corporate diplomacy.

Communicate More Formally

The good news about moving up is that you get a broader view of the business and more latitude to shape it. The bad news is that you are farther from the front lines and more likely to receive filtered information as a result. "Now, folks shield me from information that I ordinarily would have received in my old job," one newly promoted executive told me.

To avoid this, you'll need to establish alternative communication channels. You might maintain regular, direct contact with customers and select front-line employees, for instance, or create formal protocols so people at lower levels can raise serious legal or ethical concerns—all without undermining the integrity of the chain of command, of course.

You'll also need to establish new, more formal channels for communicating your strategic intent and vision across the organization—convening town hall–style meetings rather than individual or small-group sessions, or using e-mails and video more frequently to broadcast your messages to the widest possible audiences. Your direct reports may also end up playing a greater role in the spread of critical information—something to remember when you're evaluating the team members you have inherited and the leadership and communication qualities they possess.

Adjust to Greater Visibility

"All the world's a stage," as William Shakespeare put it so aptly in the play *As You Like It*, "and all the men and women merely players: They have their exits and their entrances; and one man in his time plays many parts."[4] One inescapable reality of promotion is that you inevitably attract much more attention and a higher level of scrutiny. You become the lead actor, so to speak, in a very important public play. Private moments become precious and few, and there is mounting pressure to exhibit the right kind of leadership presence, all the time. Spontaneity goes out the window—which Bert learned when his colleague in HR cautioned him against simply raising interesting ideas during team meetings.

That's why it's important to get an early fix on what "leadership presence" actually means within your new role: What does a leader look like at your level in the hierarchy? How does he or she act? What kind of spin do *you* want to put on the role? How will you make it your own? These are critical considerations, worth taking the time to explore. "Remember," one senior executive told a group of recently promoted VPs, "you are the people that your direct reports are talking about at dinner every night."

Level-Specific Competencies

Besides the common challenges associated with being promoted, there are level-specific hurdles to overcome and associated competencies to develop. Again, you'll increase your odds of making a successful transition if you can master the new skills required in your new role and let go of some of the behaviors that made you successful previously but that might not work as well in your new job.

How do competencies shift as you get promoted? In *The Leadership Pipeline*, management researchers Ram Charan, Stephen

Drotter, and James Noel focused on this question. Building on the Critical Career Crossroads framework developed by Walter Mahler in the 1970s and implemented at General Electric, they developed a model of competencies focusing on seven levels: managing oneself, managing others, managing managers, the functional manager, the business manager, the group manager, and the enterprise manager. A modified version of Charan, Drotter, and Noel's framework is summarized in figure 1-2.[5] At each level, there are skills to acquire or maintain. I've also added some common, level-specific traps to avoid.

There also is a hidden dimension to the competency shifts new leaders face as they rise through the ranks that wasn't explored by

FIGURE 1-2

Level-specific competencies and traps

		Central competencies	Common traps
More skills ↑ ↓ More mindshifts	**Front-line supervisor**	Knows the fundamentals of performance management: goal setting, oversight, feedback, coaching. Selects and develops individual contributors.	Relies too much on technical expertise. Continues to function as a "super peer" rather than a boss.
	Manager of supervisors	Knows how to set goals effectively. Delegates management responsibility. Selects and develops managers rather than individual contributors.	Relies too much on technical expertise. Is unable to delegate effectively.
	Function leader (typically a VP)	Leads the function as part of the whole business. Participates in the formulation and implementation of strategy. Selects and develops managers.	Focuses too much on the function, and not enough on the business. Focuses too much on the tactical, and not enough on the strategic.

FIGURE 1-2   (continued)

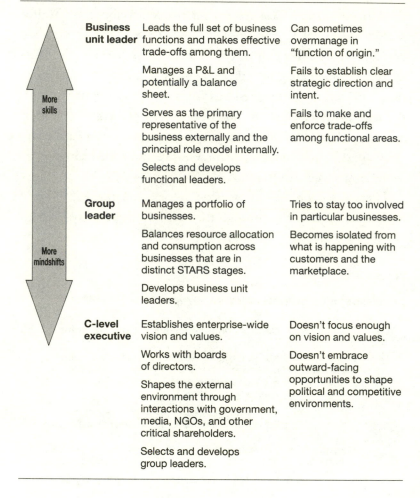

Business unit leader	Leads the full set of business functions and makes effective trade-offs among them.	Can sometimes overmanage in "function of origin."
	Manages a P&L and potentially a balance sheet.	Fails to establish clear strategic direction and intent.
	Serves as the primary representative of the business externally and the principal role model internally.	Fails to make and enforce trade-offs among functional areas.
	Selects and develops functional leaders.	
Group leader	Manages a portfolio of businesses.	Tries to stay too involved in particular businesses.
	Balances resource allocation and consumption across businesses that are in distinct STARS stages.	Becomes isolated from what is happening with customers and the marketplace.
	Develops business unit leaders.	
C-level executive	Establishes enterprise-wide vision and values.	Doesn't focus enough on vision and values.
	Works with boards of directors.	Doesn't embrace outward-facing opportunities to shape political and competitive environments.
	Shapes the external environment through interactions with government, media, NGOs, and other critical shareholders.	
	Selects and develops group leaders.	

Charan and his colleagues. Put simply, it's the move from managerial science to leadership art. Consider that the skills required of lower-level managers can often be reduced to rules and procedures. The basics of effective supervision, for example, have been well understood for decades and lend themselves brilliantly to conventional classroom training. As one rises through the hierarchy, however, the requirements for promotion can be less cut and dried, involving capabilities such as effective pattern recognition, the ability to make clear and quick judgments, or soft-side skills such as political and emotional intelligence. When examined through this lens, higher-level promotions become less about acquiring specific skills and more about making the right shifts in mind-set—for example, thinking more strategically about business problems and understanding how to shape the competitive and political environments in which the organization operates.

I've surveyed leaders participating in general-management programs at leading business schools and asked them to identify the toughest job transitions they have experienced. Their top two responses were "becoming a supervisor for the first time" and "becoming a business unit leader for the first time."[6] In the next section, I'll take a closer look at the changes in mind-set required to make this management leap and how competency models can help shape leadership development within organizations.

Becoming a Business Unit Leader

Based on more than seventy-five interviews with newly appointed business unit leaders, experienced line executives charged with developing next-generation talent, and senior HR managers, I developed a competency model consisting of seven seismic shifts that functional leaders must make to become effective business unit leaders.[7] They are as follows:

1. *From specialist to generalist.* A company's business functions are managerial subcultures with their own rules and languages. Executives transitioning to business unit leader roles must therefore work hard to achieve something I call "cross-functional fluency." Someone who

grew up in marketing obviously cannot become a native speaker of operations or R&D, but he can become fluent—familiarizing himself with the central terms, tools, and ideas employed by the various functions whose work he must integrate with the rest of the unit. The new unit head must know enough to be able to evaluate and recruit the right people to lead in the functional areas he himself is not expert in. While Bert Vandervliet had deep experience in sales and marketing and some exposure to manufacturing, for example, he had a lot to learn about R&D in order to be effective.

2. *From analyst to integrator.* The primary responsibility of functional leaders is to develop and manage their people to achieve analytical depth in relatively narrow, focused domains. By contrast, business unit leaders manage cross-functional teams with the goal of integrating the collective knowledge and using it to solve important organizational problems. As you might imagine, then, it's important for new business unit leaders to make the shift to managing integrative decision making and problem solving and, even more important, to learn how to make appropriate trade-offs. Business unit leaders must also manage in the "white spaces"—accepting responsibility for issues that don't fall neatly into any one function but are still important to the business. For Bert Vandervliet, it was a particular challenge to learn to make the necessary trade-offs across functions.

3. *From tactician to strategist.* More so than functional vice presidents, business unit leaders establish and communicate strategic direction for their organizations. So they must be able to define and clearly communicate the

mission and goals (what), the core capabilities (who), the strategy (how), and the vision (why) for their businesses. Additionally, they must be able to switch gears with ease, seamlessly shifting between tactical focus (the trees) and strategic focus (the forest). Critically, they must learn to *think strategically*, by which I mean honing their ability to (1) perceive important patterns in complex, noisy environments, (2) crystallize and communicate those patterns to others in the organization in powerful, simple ways, and (3) use these insights to anticipate and shape the reactions of other key "players," including customers and competitors.

4. *From bricklayer to architect.* As managers move up in the hierarchy, they become increasingly responsible for laying the foundations for superior performance— creating the organizational context in which business breakthroughs can happen. To be effective in this regard, business unit leaders must understand where and how strategy, structure, systems, processes, and skill bases all interact. They must also be expert in the principles of organizational design, business process improvement, and skills development and management. Like Bert Vandervliet, few high-potential leaders get any formal training in organizational development theory and practice, leaving them ill-equipped to be the architects of the organizations or to be educated consumers of the work of organizational development consultants. (For more details on how to do this, see chapter 6, "The Turnaround Challenge.")

5. *From warrior to diplomat.* Effective business unit leaders see the benefits in actively shaping the external

environment and managing critical relationships with powerful outside constituencies, including governments, NGOs, the media, and investors. They identify opportunities for cross-company collaboration, reaching out to rivals to help shape the rules of the game. Functional managers, by contrast, tend to be more focused on developing and deploying internal capabilities to compete more effectively. (For more details on how to do this, see chapter 3, "The Corporate Diplomacy Challenge.")

6. *From problem solver to problem finder.* Many leaders are promoted on the strength of their problem-solving skills. But when they reach business unit leader status, they must focus less on fixing problems and *more on recognizing and preventing what I call predictable surprises* from occurring in the first place.[8] Being a problem finder means identifying and prioritizing emerging threats, and communicating them in ways that the organization can respond to. The rest of the task calls for mobilizing preventive action and driving organizational change. And it ultimately means creating a learning organization that responds effectively to shifts in its environment and can generate surprises for its competitors. (For more details on how to do this, see chapter 7, "The Realignment Challenge.")

7. *From role holder to role model.* People in the business look first to the business unit leader for cues about the "right" behaviors and attitudes, and for vision and inspiration. At the functional leader level, it's considered acceptable just to be an efficient, effective manager,

a "role holder" if you will. Business unit leaders, by contrast, are constantly "on stage," being held to a higher standard—that of exemplary role model. For good or ill, the senior leadership of every organization is infectious. By this I mean that leaders' behaviors tend to be transmitted to their direct reports, who pass them on to the next level, and so on down through their organizations. Over time, they permeate the organization from top to bottom, influencing activity at all levels. Eventually they become embodied in the organizational culture, influencing the types of people who get promoted and hired into the organization, creating a self-reinforcing feedback loop—either positive or negative.

Like most new business unit leaders, Bert Vandervliet confronted the need to make all seven of these seismic shifts in tandem. He had to learn more about unfamiliar functions, focus more on integrative problem solving, think more strategically, make some key organizational design choices, conduct effective diplomacy, prevent predictable surprises, and be the most important role model for his business. That's what makes that first appointment to lead a business so challenging. Fortunately Bert also had some important resources, both within himself and in the organization, to help him make the leap.

Meeting the Personal Adaptive Challenge

With every promotion, you confront the common core challenges anew, as well as the shifts in level-specific competencies required for success. Together, these define the personal adaptive challenges you face in your new role. As discussed in the introduction, there are a handful of things that you can do to accelerate your personal adjustment to any new leadership role: assessing your strengths and weaknesses given the situation, disciplining yourself to do things that don't come naturally, building a complementary team, and leveraging wise counsel.

A look at Bert Vandervliet's developmental history, for instance, suggests that he needs to acquire deeper functional fluency in operations and R&D—a process that might not be comfortable for him but that he needs to undertake nonetheless. He should also take his HR colleague's advice to heart and confront the possibility that his overmanagement of his vice president of sales and marketing is a symptom of his own insecurities rather than a true reflection of his direct report's capabilities.

Then there is the question of who can help Bert to better delegate the work that needs to be done. Given that he needs to focus more on the outside and has deep marketing and sales expertise, it may make sense for him to forge a working partnership with someone who can function as a chief operating officer for the business; likely candidates might be his vice presidents of operations and finance.

Finally, Bert needs to recognize that the advice network that served him well as a functional VP probably won't be enough to support his needs as a business unit leader. He needs to cultivate more wise counselors who can help him gain additional insight into the important functions where he is weak, better understand what it takes to run a business as a whole, advise him on managing the internal and external political challenges he confronts, and help him prepare for the next level. So in the midst of all the other challenges he faces, he must devote the time to thinking about and realigning his network of advisors and counselors.

Accelerating Development

Beyond adopting a common framework and tools for accelerating every promotion transition (discussed in-depth in the conclusion, "Designing Companywide Transition-Acceleration Systems"), what can your company do to help you when you get promoted? First off, they should build and use *good competency models*—definitions of the skills required of leaders at different levels—tuned to the company's leadership pipeline. Done well, these will give you good guidance about what you need to go to the next level.

To be truly useful, these models should be real, simple, and executable. Realism is important: managers are told advancement is likely to come if they can develop the stated competencies in the model. But if you buy into the system, invest the time, and develop the competencies, and promotions still aren't forthcoming (and there are many reasons why this could be the case; for example, because advancement in the company actually depends on support from political networks), the model will do little but breed cynicism. So companies need to give careful thought to how they will adopt and deploy competency models.

Simplicity is critical for ensuring that competency models are actually implemented. If there are a thousand and one skills, requirements, or characteristics listed—or if they are too complex or ambiguous—aspiring leaders won't know where to focus. Likewise, it will be difficult for talent-development professionals in the company to figure out how to use and support the model. Instead, the model should comprise a reasonably compact set of skills, characteristics, and the like. If you have more than ten for a given level, you're certainly in trouble.

Finally, there's the issue of implementation. A competency model is worth little if you can't evaluate baseline levels of performance and translate your findings into programs or projects that can help individuals improve. So before you implement any kind of competency model, make sure it's supported by robust assessment tools.

Beware, however, of engaging in cross-company or cross-industry comparisons of scores: such benchmarks can't control for the differences in companies' strategies, cultures, and incentives. I saw this happen when a leading assessment consulting firm evaluated the talent at the highest levels of the number one company in a global transportation industry. The mean strategic thinking score for senior leaders was far below the benchmarked cross-industry baseline—which rightly stirred up indignation and undercut the credibility of the competency model and assessment process. What hadn't been factored into the process was company culture, which, because of the nature of the business, placed a very great emphasis on execution and operational efficiency.

The other major way that companies can help ensure successful promotion transitions is by creating career-development pathways consisting of the right types of experiences. Artfully designed pathways can accelerate companies' ability to build deep benches of leadership talent. The one BSC set up for Bert Vandervliet provides a good example. Bert was guided through a series of positions, each with a designated purpose, which offered him valuable lessons in four important career-development dimensions:

1. Development in his core function and exposure to other functions.

2. Understanding of the company's range of businesses.

3. Home country and international assignments.

4. Business unit and corporate assignments.

Note that this mix of assignments made sense given the nature of BSC's business—diversified, global, and decentralized. The mix in another company could obviously be quite different, depending on its own characteristics.

BSC used several approaches for designing its development pathways, the first one being its deployment of *stepping-stones*—the thoughtful design of a sequence of assignments, each of which represents a significant stretch along one or two of the critical development dimensions but not so much of a stretch that the leader slips and falls. In a well-thought-out progression, Bert moved from a product-management assignment to an international assignment in business development (to which some exposure to manufacturing was subsequently added), to a more senior post in sales and marketing, to a different division, and then to a corporate HR role.

The second approach is the use of *playgrounds*—putting future general managers in charge of distinct businesses (or significant projects) that they can easily get their arms around and in which they will have the opportunity to learn what excellence looks like. The plastic resins business that Bert joined was relatively small and was in a sustaining-success situation, with a strong team in place. Think of how much more difficult it would have been for Bert if he had been thrust immediately into a much larger unit, perhaps with multiple business lines, or had been immediately confronted with a turnaround or realignment situation.

One additional assignment would have helped Bert to be even better prepared to take over as business unit leader: to run a portion of a business with a distinct P&L and with responsibility for a few critical functions. Doing this while reporting to an experienced business unit leader whom he could ask for advice would have given him deeper familiarity with the cross-functional challenge. As such, it would have been both a stepping-stone and a playground.

Bert eventually found his footing in his first business unit leader role. Three years later he became business unit leader of

BSC's high-growth nutritionals business unit. This gave Bert experience in pharmaceuticals, another of the company's critical industry sectors, and it helped lay the foundation for his future promotion to the group leadership level.

Promotion Checklist

Lists like this one appear at the end of each chapter to help you crystallize the key lessons and apply them to your situation. Use these questions to guide your analysis and develop your transition plan. References to additional resources are available at www.YourNextMove.net.

1. What does it mean to "promote yourself" into your new role? What must you do more of, even if you don't enjoy or feel fully competent doing it? What do you need to do less of or let go?

2. Which of the common promotion challenges—balancing breadth and depth, delegating more deeply, influencing differently, communicating more formally, and adjusting to greater visibility—do you most need to focus on?

3. Which level-specific competencies do you need to develop to be successful at the new level?

4. What can your organization do to help you accelerate your development?

5. What do you need to do to meet the personal adaptive challenge? Do you need to enhance your self-awareness

and, if so, in what ways? Do you need to exert discipline
to do things that don't come comfortably? Do you
need to identify or recruit natural complements in
your team? Do you need to alter your advice network
or use it differently?

2 The Leading-Former-Peers Challenge

JULIA MARTINEZ'S PROMOTION TO DIRECTOR OF MARKETING at Alpha Telecommunications took her former peers, many of whom would now be her direct reports, by surprise. Julia's boss and mentor, Thomas Collins, was good at many things, but communicating about people issues was not one of them. Within a week of being promoted to vice president of sales and marketing at the midsize telecom services company, he appointed Julia, one of the five marketing managers who had reported to him, to be his successor.

Julia inherited an organization that had made impressive strides in the past few years, a primary reason for her boss's promotion. Effective marketing had helped propel Alpha to a leading position in providing specialized telecommunications services for small businesses. At the same time, the company was facing increasing competition from several well-funded start-ups. These emerging rivals, in an effort to build market share, had priced their services to undercut Alpha. Forced to respond with price reductions of its own, Alpha had begun to experience pressure on its operating margins. Customer retention also was becoming an issue because of the intensifying competition, even as new acquisitions were showing signs of slowing.

Julia had been convinced for some time that Alpha needed to change its marketing strategy. Rather than engage in the "broadcast" approach that Collins had adopted, she thought Alpha needed to sharpen its focus: identify the most attractive market segments and create targeted campaigns to reach customers in those groups. She also thought that the organization should shift its resources from customer acquisition to customer retention and brand building. Finally, she was concerned that too many projects were under way to develop potential new service offerings, and that they were insufficiently grounded in solid market research.

Collins was preoccupied with his own transition (the previous VP of marketing had left unexpectedly to join another company), and Julia hadn't had time to discuss goals and expectations with him. But she was confident she could sell him on the new direction. After all, Collins had hired her into Alpha. For the past three years, she had been the company's manager of marketing communications and had built a highly capable team that developed product-related materials. But Julia also boasted a strong technical background, including a master's degree in applied statistics and five years as a market research analyst at a leading consumer-products company. So she understood the power of segmentation and was confident she knew how to implement it.

Julia did have some concerns about her new team, however. First, there was Andy, a talented if somewhat ego-driven leader in marketing strategy. He had viewed himself as the logical candidate for advancement. Julia knew that her promotion had been a blow to him, and she wondered if he'd be able to get over his disappointment and work effectively under her direction. If she could bring him on board, Andy could be an important asset and ally in pursuing her new ideas. But the last thing Julia needed was a resentful former peer undermining what she was trying to do.

Another team member, Amanda, posed a different challenge: as a manager of marketing support, Amanda had done a solid job in terms of overseeing projects and driving execution. But she was not a particularly inspiring leader, nor perhaps was she the person Julia needed in that role if she were to implement her new strategy. Over the years, Amanda had often sought Julia's personal and professional advice; they had become, if not friends, something more than business colleagues. Now Julia would be the one evaluating Amanda's performance.

In addition, Julia planned to manage her team differently than Collins had. He was very hands-on, a style that suited him. Julia, by contrast, preferred to vest more authority with the members of her team and to encourage shared commitment and collective accountability to the greatest extent possible. With all that in mind, as soon as the schedule allowed, she planned to take her team off-site for a one-day situation assessment and strategy discussion.

Finally, Julia was somewhat apprehensive about trading her old peer group for a new one. Many of the people she'd now be interacting with day to day were significantly older and more experienced than she was. Some had a lot of influence in the organization, and one had been a candidate for the VP position Collins was moving to. Now she was just the new kid on the block, and Collins's kid at that. Julia wondered how best to engage with her new peer group during her transition.

All these concerns crystallized for Julia the day after her promotion was announced: she went to the cafeteria to get lunch, as she usually did. When she entered the seating area, she saw her new peers eating together at one table and several of her former peers sitting at another. Suddenly the dining tray felt heavy in her arms.

The Leading-Former-Peers Challenge

If it hasn't already happened, it is very likely that you will experience the challenge of leading former peers at some point in your career. Most business leaders do; many go through it multiple times as they climb the corporate ladder. But too many learn to make this challenging transition through trial and error. They make predictable mistakes, such as not establishing sufficient authority with their new teams or not understanding that their relationship with their boss must change. They learn hard lessons and apply them in future transitions, but this is an inefficient, wasteful process.

One scene in Shakespeare's *Henry IV* (act V, scene 5) brilliantly captures the tensions leaders face when they are promoted in their organizations. Henry is the Crown Prince of England, destined to inherit the throne, but he spends much of his youth partying with disreputable characters, in particular the drunken Falstaff and his cronies. His father dies, and Henry is to be crowned king. During the coronation scene, Henry very publicly rejects Falstaff— "I know thee not, old man. Fall to thy prayers."—and sees firsthand how this slight hurts his old friend. This exchange signifies the major shift Henry makes from dissolute youth to one of the great rulers of England: his role changed dramatically and, as a result, so did many of his long-standing relationships.

A similar shift takes place when executives ascend to higher positions within their organizations: when you're promoted to lead the people with whom you formerly worked side by side, the nature of your interactions with those individuals will change in important ways. And, in most cases, new leaders are left to figure out how to navigate these psychosocial challenges on their own—as Julia Martinez was.

Chapter 1 of this book outlined the basic organizational challenges leaders face when they're promoted: How should you delegate and communicate differently? How do you balance breadth and depth in a new role? How do you develop new competencies and project the sort of presence that is appropriate for your new job?

Leaders who are promoted to lead former peers do face these challenges and it would be easy to imagine that tackling them in an environment you're familiar with would be easy. After all, you've got the lay of the land (the culture and critical players, the business and what drives it), and you've probably banked some "relationship capital" to boot.

On the contrary, being promoted to lead people who were formerly your peers is among the *toughest* transitions you can make, precisely because of the complex web of organizational relationships you've created over the years and must now redefine—with your boss, former peers, and new peers. You think you know everyone, and everyone thinks they know you. *But those relationships were shaped, in part, by the roles you previously played. The protocols, perceptions, and interactions must all be different now.*

Relationship Reengineering

The imperative for Julia Martinez—and for all leaders who find themselves moving up and having to lead their former peers—is to engage in what I like to call "relationship reengineering." Global businesses often try to improve their odds of success by fundamentally reengineering processes to meet their changing needs. Similarly, transitioning executives can improve their chances of realizing positive change by redefining their relationships in light of shifting roles. Doing this means focusing hard on your interactions with critical people, understanding how those relationships need to change, and developing a plan for making the necessary shifts. Specifically, you should try to adhere to the following basic principles:

- Accept that relationships have to change.

- Focus early on rites of passage.

- Reenlist your (good) former peers.

- Establish your authority deftly.

- Focus on what's good for the business.

- Approach team building with caution.

Accept That Relationships Have to Change

In the process of working together for long periods and facing down shared challenges, work colleagues can become friends, or something close to it. An unfortunate price of promotion, however, is that your personal relationships with former peers must become less so. Close personal relationships and effective supervisory ones are rarely compatible, for several important reasons. First, you can't afford to have your judgments about important business issues clouded by your personal feelings about the players involved. And second, you can't allow the perception to take hold among the members of your team that you play favorites.

In the early months of her tenure, Julia could very well find herself sitting across the table from Amanda, needing to deliver hard-edged performance feedback but experiencing a desire to cushion the hurt. If she succumbs to the temptation to go easy,

Julia could undermine not only the company's performance but her own leadership. If she does what's right for the business, she will irreversibly alter the relationship, and she will see it in Amanda's eyes. There is a right answer, but that doesn't make it easy. Julia should take care to send a consistent message to everyone from the start: "I will be fair in my evaluation of you." Then, of course, she has to live up to this by translating the rhetoric into action on a consistent basis.

Focus Early on Rites of Passage

Those first days of an internal promotion are more about symbolism than substance. Indeed, certain rites of passage can help to establish the new leader and, hence, simplify the relationship reengineering that must be done. In an ideal world, Julia's boss, Thomas Collins, would have set the stage for her promotion—specifically, meeting privately with Andy to share his reasons for promoting Julia and then calling the team together to announce his successor. This would have laid the groundwork for Julia to transition smoothly into her new role.

It also would have helped if the company had had a solid process for communicating about internal promotions. This means formal and informal messages sent to all employees about the selection process and outcomes. In doing this, it's important to give attention not just to content but also to timing. In one organization I worked with, all formal promotion announcements were communicated via e-mail in the late morning. This meant that people had time to absorb the implications and perhaps talk about the promotion over lunch. It also gave the newly promoted leader time to reach out to key stakeholders on the same day, participate in a short meeting with available members of the new team, and begin to initiate one-on-one meetings.

It didn't unfold this way for Julia, however, so she has to write her own "coronation scene," so to speak. This should include convening her team for a short meeting—essentially, providing a chance for everyone to acknowledge publicly that a shift has occurred. Julia should carefully draft a short script around a few central messages: that she is looking forward to working with the team to move the organization forward, that she values all team members' contributions, and that she is looking forward to meeting with each of them individually. (Ideally, she would have already begun setting up those meetings.)

Reenlist Your (Good) Former Peers

Behind every "happy" promotion are the one or more ambitious souls who wanted the job but didn't get it. As much as practical, companies should prepare the people who are not going to get promoted. The ability to do this is rooted, in part, in performance review and succession systems that do a rigorous job of evaluating performance and, critically, that shape realistic expectations about the potential for advancement.

If the promotion process is managed well, the final choice for the position will almost certainly disappoint some—but it should never be a surprise. More often than not, however, newly promoted leaders like Julia have to deal with former peers who may feel dejected, angry, or even victimized. Some will be able to get past their disappointments to support your initiatives for getting things done; you'll need to find ways to reenlist these former peers.

You'll of course need to recognize that disappointed competitors will go through stages of grieving similar to those defined by psychiatrist Elisabeth Kübler-Ross (denial, anger, bargaining, depression, and acceptance) and that it will take some time for them to work through these feelings.[1] If your former peers are good and you want to keep them, then you should respect this and do what you can to help the adjustment process along. A good first step is to communicate and reinforce that you recognize what people have contributed to your organization's success to that point. This is probably best done privately unless there is an authentic moment when you can do so publicly. Otherwise it's easy to come across as condescending.

You also should think hard about whether and how best to engage with disappointed direct reports more directly about what they are experiencing. Should you talk with them right away or after they've had more time to process the change? Should you address their concerns directly or obliquely? Should you be empathetic or matter-of-fact in your communications? It really depends on the person and your relationship with them. If they are disappointed but not resentful, comfortable talking about such things, and you have a good relationship with them, then it can be effective to directly address the issue. If, as was the case with Julia and Andy, they harbor some bad feeling or are uncomfortable openly discussing such things, then it's probably best to leave the ball in their court, while at the same time signaling that they are valued members of the team.

If and when you do have these discussions, remember that your former peers' concerns about their careers—and associated fears that they have been dead-ended—will probably rank high on their lists of priorities. It's easy for them to interpret your promotion as an implicit criticism of their abilities and potential. So if you can genuinely help to alleviate those concerns, then you should. For instance, if Julia can credibly sit down with Andy and convince him that she is committed to helping him develop and advance, she may have a good chance of reenlisting him and building a critical new direct-report relationship.

Keep in mind, though, that sometimes former peers simply can't get over perceived organizational or personal slights. As able as they may be, they may not be able to work for you. You'll need to keep a careful eye out to see if people are genuinely getting on board. If after a reasonable period of time they are not, then you'll need to help these individuals find other opportunities.

Establish Your Authority Deftly

To exert your authority over former peers, you have to walk the knife's edge between over- and underasserting yourself. You may be tempted to act as a sort of "superpeer"—overplaying your desire to continue coaching, encouraging, and supporting former peers despite the title change. Conversely, be careful not to develop a Napoleon complex in your new role, issuing edicts at will without realizing it.

It's critical to find the middle ground early on. For instance, Julia might consider putting on hold, at least for a little while, her plans for creating more of an empowerment culture. In those first few months, she should adopt a "consult-and-decide" approach when dealing with critical issues—in part to establish her own authority, and in part because that's what people at Alpha are used to. By listening carefully (the consult side of the equation), she'll demonstrate to her new team that she values thoughtful input. By considering carefully and coming to resolution quickly (the decide piece of the equation), she'll convey both that she is capable of smart decisions and ultimately accountable for results. Once Julia has established a new rhythm with the team, she can engage them in more consensus building if and when it's appropriate.

Focus on What's Good for the Business

From the moment your appointment is announced, some former peers, now direct reports, will be straining to discern whether you will play favorites or seek to advance your political agenda at their expense. One antidote to this potentially disruptive dynamic is adopting a relentless, principled focus on doing what is right for the business. Every decision you make should be framed in those terms—so long as you're genuinely committed to this ethic and prepared to live with the consequences. The sooner your new direct reports see that you'll be "hard on issues and soft on people," the better.

A related way to immunize yourself against perceptions that you are playing politics in leading former peers is to adopt what INSEAD professors W. Chan Kim and Renée Mauborgne have termed a "fair process" for making important decisions.[2] This means establishing and upholding work processes that are perceived as just—for example, by melding consult-and-decide decision making with "put the interests of the business first" criteria for evaluating alternative courses of action.

A few months into her new role, Julia was able to apply these principles to help rationalize the many projects that were underway at Alpha to develop new service offerings. Although many other parts of the organization were involved in new product development, the marketing strategy component was Andy's responsibility. Julia knew that any effort to shift the strategy would be a political minefield, not just because of Andy, but because it touched so many sets of interests and agendas in the company. So rather that attack the issue head on, she decided to set up a project evaluation team and put Andy in charge of it (he responded well to the opportunity for visibility). She was able to leverage the relationships she had built outside her organization to staff the team with capable people from sales, operations, and finance.

Critically, she specified in detail the multistage process the team would use to conduct the evaluation. The first stage was a thorough review of existing market research that resulted in the commissioning of a new study to clarify what customers were really looking for. In the next stage, she directed the team to craft qualitative and quantitative criteria for evaluating the costs and benefits of each project. Only then did she have the team assess the existing project portfolio. By this point, no one was disputing the need for significant rationalization, and agreement on what to continue and what to stop was reasonably easy to reach.

Approach Team Building with Caution

The lure of the off-site meeting is strong for many newly promoted leaders. Like Julia Martinez, they have agendas they want to pursue and teams they want to mobilize. "Just let me get everyone together in a quiet place, give me their undivided attention, and we can move mountains," goes the logic.

No question, an off-site can be a powerful vehicle for mobilizing change. Done right, the meeting can focus people's attention, break down barriers, build commitment, and leave teams energized, aligned, and ready to do great things. But poorly planned and facilitated, such a meeting can go very badly. In a worst-case scenario, conflicts are exacerbated, opposing coalitions are empowered, and the new leader's authority is undermined from the get-go. (See the box "Off-Site Planning Checklist.")

Before you reflexively schedule an off-site meeting, you need to step back and answer two interrelated questions: What am I trying to accomplish? And is an off-site the best way to achieve my goals? There are a number of reasons why you'd answer no to the second query—a chief one being the risk that you'll fuel the rise of opposing coalitions. If some people are likely to resist the changes you want to make, then an early off-site may only serve to galvanize that group of dissenters, no matter how latent their objections, to the changes the organization is making. Better to start at the micro level—building support one by one and in smaller group meetings before convening an off-site.

Julia Martinez is considering convening an early off-site, ostensibly as a way to launch her attempts to shift the marketing organization's strategic direction (toward more customer segmentation) and culture (toward shared accountability). This would be a huge mistake, however. She has not laid the groundwork with her boss for creating a new strategy, nor has she established sufficient authority in her new role to introduce democracy.

If Julia decides to go ahead with an off-site, the primary objectives should be diagnosis and relationship building, rather than strategic planning. She and the members of her team can rigorously vet and analyze changes in the business environment and come to a shared understanding of the situation. The data and insights from this meeting could even give Julia the ammunition necessary to convince her boss that a strategy shift is in order. Meanwhile, the collaboration and discussion in this meeting may go a long way toward helping Julia reengineer her relationships with her former peers—showcasing her as a new leader who is firmly but judiciously in control. Once these foundations are in place, she can turn her attention to strategy and process, perhaps by holding a subsequent off-site.

Each of these principles presents its own set of unique challenges, no doubt. But your ability to successfully adopt them can help position you for success in leading former peers. You must also recognize, of course, that you'll have to grow into your new role—and that it's going to take some time.

Off-Site Planning Checklist

Setting Goals

Before you reflexively schedule an off-site for your new team, you need to clarify the reasons for doing so. In other words, what are you trying to accomplish with this meeting? There are six important reasons for convening the group off site:

- To gain a shared understanding of the business (diagnostic focus)
- To create a strategy and define the vision (strategy focus)
- To change the way the team works together (team-process focus)
- To build or alter relationships in the group (relationship focus)
- To develop a plan and commit to achieving it (planning focus)
- To address significant conflicts (conflict-resolution focus)

Getting Down to Details

If you decide that an off-site would indeed be useful for the group, start to consider the logistics of the meeting, based on your answers to the following questions:

Companies can also do a lot to accelerate the team adjustment process for those who are promoted to lead former peers. One powerful tool is the new leader assimilation process.[3] A facilitator, perhaps from HR or an external consultant for more senior managers, meets individually with the new leader and the direct reports and then brokers a joint meeting. The focus of discussions

- When and where should the meeting be held?
- Which issues will be dealt with, and in what order?
- Who should act as facilitator?

In particular, don't neglect the facilitation question. If you are a skilled facilitator and if the team respects you—and is not enmeshed in a conflict—it may make sense for you to be both leader and facilitator for the session. If not, you'd be well advised to bring in a skilled outsider—a move that will immediately signal seriousness to your team and elevate your status in their eyes.

Avoiding the Traps

- Don't try to do too much in a single off-site meeting. You can't realistically accomplish more than two of the goals outlined above in a day or two. Focus, and strive to stay focused.
- Don't put the cart before the horse. You can't try to create a strategy and define the vision without first establishing the right foundation: a shared understanding of the business environment (diagnostic focus) and workplace relationships (relationship focus).

---

is on expectations, and how the newly promoted leader plans to manage the group. (See the box "The New Leader Assimilation Process.") Done well, the process can dramatically accelerate the development of working relationships and eliminate key uncertainties that slow team development. It also provides an important rite of passage—it explicitly acknowledges that a significant shift has taken place.

The New Leader Assimilation Process

New leader assimilation processes typically involve the following steps:

1. Process overview. In a group session including the new leader and the team, the facilitator explains the purpose of a new leader assimilation session and provides an overview of the process.

2. Data collection and analysis. The facilitator interviews the new leader and each team member separately to identify the key issues/opportunities to be addressed during the assimilation session. Typical questions:

   – What do you want to know about the new leader?

   – What do you want the new leader to know about you?

The facilitator then summarizes the data while being careful to preserve anonymity to the greatest degree possible.

3. Presession meeting. The facilitator, new leader, and potentially an HR representative meet prior to the session to review the data summary and plan the assimilation session.

4. Assimilation session. The facilitator conducts the team session, typically a half day or full day, focusing on key issues and opportunities identified in the interviews. The outcome is acceleration of the building of relationships and the alignment of expectations.

Working with Your New Peers and Boss

Your relationships with your former peers are not the only ones that need to be reengineered. Like Julia Martinez, you are part of a much larger network that includes new peers and your boss. (See Julia's network in figure 2-1.)

Working with New Peers

As someone newly promoted from within, you will need to reach out to your new peer group—and interact with them as a peer would—as soon as possible. These interactions must obviously be handled with care and tact: consider that among Julia's new peers (Collins's former peers and now his direct reports), there are likely to be disappointed candidates for the VP of marketing job that Collins eventually got. Remember, too, that Julia may be viewed

FIGURE 2-1

Julia's new network

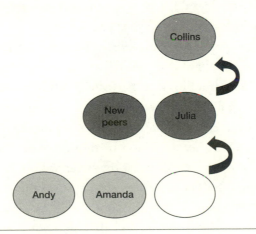

as Collins's "favored child" because he hired and developed her. So some of her new peers may even try to undermine Julia's attempts to lead change in the marketing organization simply out of frustration or to subtly call Collins's selection into question.

With such politics in mind, it's important for transitioning leaders to strike the right balance between self-assurance and cockiness in building relationships with new peers. You should set up a series of one-on-one meetings with new colleagues and strategize with your boss about how you'll be introduced at the first staff meeting.

In the one-on-one meetings, you should be asking lots of questions so as to understand the web of explicit and implicit alliances in your new peer group: how can you help your new peers achieve their important goals, and how can they help you? In staff meetings, the right approach early on is usually to listen and respond thoughtfully. As you gain a better understanding of the alliances and culture, and, importantly, build some relationship capital, you can begin to participate more actively. For instance, in Julia's case, she is younger and less experienced than her peers. She needs to build some credibility with them in her new role. So while it would be a mistake for her to try too hard to prove herself early on, so, too, would it be wrong of her not to "come to the table" after she's gotten up to speed a bit.

Speaking of coming to the table, let's reconsider Julia's cafeteria conundrum: should she sit with her old peers, her new peers, or turn tail and head back to her office? Withdrawing from the situation is definitely the wrong answer (although that's what happened in the real situation); Julia would miss a valuable opportunity to set her transition in motion. The "right" answer depends in part on the culture of the organization. It could make sense, however, for her to at least stop by the table with her new peers, say hello, and mention that she will be reaching out to meet with them individually, and that she's looking forward to working more closely with them. Given the informal social setting of the cafeteria, it probably doesn't make sense for Julia to insert herself into that gathering—and it might send the wrong signals to her former peers. She could comfortably sit with the members of her old peer group, however.

Working with Your Boss

The trap here is assuming that just because you and your boss are the same people, the relationship will stay the same. Just as your relationships with your former peers will change when you're promoted internally, so will your interactions with your boss. Shifting roles mean shifting expectations—and different "best" ways of working with one another. Simply put, as you make the transition to a new role, you'll need to cast off long-held assumptions and adapt your relationship with your boss to meet the needs of both your changed roles.

In Julia's case, she's making some potentially dangerous assumptions about how receptive Collins might be to her plan to alter Alpha's marketing strategy. She needs to meet with him as soon as possible to review the situation and his expectations. If she really believes a shift in strategy is necessary, she should gather her data and prepare her arguments—presenting her ideas in a way that doesn't suggest she's criticizing what came before.

Julia also needs to be attuned to the realities of Collins's own transition: he, too, has been promoted to lead former peers. How well Julia integrates herself with his old peer group will unquestionably reflect on him, good or bad. She is in a position to help him achieve some early wins in his new role, so she should give some thought as to how she might support him in this way.

Finally, there will inevitably be disagreements about how to "be" the marketing director—Julia's new title, Collins's old one. He would be right to believe that he knows more about how to do that job than she does. The risk, of course, is that he will try to continue to do Julia's new job. If his transition is going well, Collins probably will be too busy, even if that is his inclination. But if he is struggling in his new role, he may try to retreat to his comfort zone.

In summary, the challenge of leading former peers is always fraught with difficulty. After some initial struggles, Julia was ultimately able to find her footing in her new role. The relationship with Andy was never developed into a fully productive one. After eight months, he left to join a start-up in a marketing director role.

Leading-Former-Peers Checklist

1. How is the network of relationships that you need to succeed in your new role different? Who are the key new people with whom you must build relationships? How must relationships change with your former peers, new peers, and boss?

2. What are the key rites of passage that signify you have been promoted and how should you prepare for them? What additional things might you or your boss do to signal that a significant shift is taking place?

3. What should you do to help speed up the process of adjustment for your former peers now that you will be leading them? How should you approach reenlisting the talented people in your organization?

4. How should you approach establishing your authority? How will you achieve the right balance between being in charge and empowering your team?

5. What formal team-building work will you do, if any? What is the right timing and focus for early team interactions?

6. How will you approach building relationships with your new peers? At what point will you shift from more of an early observational mode to becoming an active member of that team?

7. If you have the same boss, how will that relationship need to change given the new roles you both are playing? How will you approach surfacing and discussing the needed shifts?

3 The Corporate Diplomacy Challenge

AFTER JUST FOUR MONTHS IN HER NEW JOB AT VAN LEAR Foods, Irina Petrenko was deeply frustrated by the bureaucratic maneuvering going on at the corporate-headquarters level. "Where's the support?" she wondered. An accomplished sales and marketing professional, Irina had risen through the country-management ranks of Van Lear, a leading international food company, to become the firm's managing director (also known as "country manager") in her native Ukraine. She was a hard-driving, results-oriented executive who had overseen dramatic growth in her territory.

Based on this success, Irina was promoted to managing director and assigned to turn around the company's struggling operations in the Balkans. She thrived in this complex multinational environment, bringing in new talent, adjusting the product mix, changing the packaging to better match customers' preferences and budgets, streamlining operations, and executing a targeted acquisition. Two and a half years later, the Balkans business was on track to achieving sustained double-digit growth.

Senior leadership at Van Lear recognized the potential executive talent they had in Irina and decided she needed some regional experience to round out her portfolio of accomplishments. So they appointed her regional vice president of marketing. In this new role, Irina would oversee marketing strategy, branding, and new product development for Van Lear's country operations in Europe, the Middle East, and Africa (the EMEA region). Her new home base was Van Lear's EMEA headquarters, located near Geneva, Switzerland. Irina would report directly to Marjorie Aaron, the senior vice president of corporate marketing, who was based at the company's U.S. headquarters. Irina also had a dotted-line reporting relationship with her former boss, Harald Emberger, the international vice president for EMEA operations, to whom all the country managers (all managing directors) reported.

Irina dug into her new role with her usual conviction and enthusiasm. She conducted a thorough review of current affairs, including a series of one-on-one conversations with managing directors across the EMEA region and with her former boss. She also traveled to the United States expressly to meet with her new boss and other important staff in Van Lear's marketing and R&D groups.

Drawing upon those discussions, plus her own experiences in the field, Irina concluded that Van Lear's most pressing problems—and opportunities—in the EMEA region lay in managing the tension between centralizing and decentralizing certain processes and decisions involved with new-product development. Specifically, to what degree should the company insist on consistent product formulation and packaging across the region and to what degree should it allow some flexibility for local variations? For example, what scope should a managing director in the Middle East have to adjust the recipe for one of Van Lear's leading biscuit brands to appeal to local tastes?

Irina wasted no time putting together a presentation outlining the results of her initial assessment along with recommendations for improvements. Her suggestions included increasing centralization in some areas (for example, decisions concerning overall brand identity and positioning) and giving the managing directors more flexibility in others (such as the ability to make limited adjustments to recipes). Then she scheduled individual meetings with Marjorie and Harald, who both listened attentively and saw the merits of her approach. The next step, they advised, would be to brief the stakeholders who would be most affected by this organizational change—Van Lear's corporate R&D and marketing executives in the United States and its country managers in the EMEA region.

Irina had been heartened by her bosses' positive responses. Six weeks and several confounding meetings later, however, she felt like she was caught in quicksand. Following up on Marjorie's mandate, she had scheduled a meeting with David Wallace, the corporate senior vice president of R&D, his staff, and important members of Van Lear's corporate marketing team. She then flew to the United States to present to a group of more than thirty people, drawn from the main areas of R&D and marketing. Virtually every one of them had suggestions to offer, most of which would result in more centralization, not less. It also became clear to Irina during the course of the meeting—watching the body language and listening to the pointed comments—that there were significant tensions between corporate R&D and marketing. "I've walked into a political minefield," she thought. Irina came away from the meeting with a greater appreciation for her predecessor, with whom she'd had frequent clashes when she was a country managing director. Clearly, he'd been grappling with a lot more at the headquarters level than she'd realized.

To her surprise, the conference call with the EMEA country managers—her old colleagues—didn't go much better. They were, of course, more than happy to accept any ideas Irina had for creating additional flexibility. But when there was any mention of limits to their autonomy, the group rapidly closed ranks. One respected managing director, Rolf Eiklid, expressed concern that even if they did agree to some forms of centralization, the flexibility they received in return wouldn't be enough to compensate for what they would be giving up. Because country managers had P&L responsibility for their territories and significant latitude to allocate local resources, Irina knew all too well that they could not be forced to fall in line.

The usually sure-footed Irina was thrown off her stride by this recent turn of events. She was used to operating with more authority and more urgency to get things done. The political maneuvering she had encountered at headquarters was dispiriting; so was the lack of support from her former colleagues. She was left wondering whether she had the patience and finesse to navigate the politics of her new regional role.

The Corporate Diplomacy Challenge

Irina Petrenko's dilemma is a fairly common one for line leaders who move into positions where getting things done suddenly depends more on influence (your ability to build coalitions of support) rather than authority (your place in the hierarchy). The essential challenge is the same whether your new role involves navigating within a "matrix" organization (as was the case for Irina); negotiating with powerful external parties, such as government agencies; or leading a critical support function, such as HR or IT, but having other functions control critical budgets. If you want to achieve your objectives, you need to learn how to practice *corporate diplomacy*—effectively leveraging organizational alliances, networks, and other business relationships in order to get things done.

Failure to master this critical skill can lead to trouble: it's easy for leaders who are used to wielding authority (and making decisions with their place in the hierarchy in mind) to get frustrated and attempt to impel people to do what they want. Instead of overcoming resistance, these leaders end up catalyzing *reactive coalition building*; they prompt potential opponents to build alliances—and reflexively close the ranks, as Irina's former colleagues did. Indeed, the new leader can get caught in a deeply debilitating cycle in which her overreliance on authority yields increasing opposition, which then prompts even more inflexibility from the leader, and so on. Left unchecked, the result can be a series of increasingly polarizing conflicts between the new leader and important players in the organization. The new leader is particularly vulnerable in these battles; she still doesn't understand how the organization works and hasn't yet established alliances of her own, so these are fights she is unlikely to win.

Becoming an Effective Diplomat

What does it mean to be an effective corporate diplomat? Great diplomats proceed from the assumption that supportive alliances must be built in order to get anything serious done in organizations. They understand that opposition to change is likely, so they anticipate and develop strategies for surmounting it. They don't expect to win over everyone; instead they focus on creating a critical mass of support. Most important, they devote as much energy to figuring out *how* to do things as they do to understanding *what* should be done. The starting point is to understand the importance of laying the foundation for alliances and defining key influence objectives.

Laying the Foundations for Alliances

Early on, transitioning leaders put a lot of effort into cultivating relationships in their new organizations, believing that these connections will pay off when it comes time to get things done—which is true. It's wise for new leaders to build new relationships in anticipation of future needs. After all, you'd never want to be meeting your neighbors for the first time in the middle of the night while your house is burning down. But this operating philosophy underemphasizes an important point about organizational politics—namely, that there is a difference between building relationships and building alliances.

In a nutshell, *alliances* are explicit or implicit agreements between two or more parties to jointly pursue specific agendas. By contrast, *relationships* comprise a broader class of social interactions, including personal friendships, which may or may not involve agreements to pursue specific goals.

If relationships don't necessarily imply alliances, the reverse also is true: effective corporate diplomats often build alliances with people with whom they have no significant ongoing relationships. Some alliances are founded on long-term shared interests that provide the basis for ongoing, supportive interactions; others are short-term arrangements that push specific agendas and then disband. Indeed, you may find yourself cooperating with people you usually disagree with—except, perhaps, when it comes to achieving a narrow goal involving a tiny slice of the business.

Leaders who, like Irina, are transitioning into positions where influence matters more than authority therefore need to focus as much on *understanding others' agendas and identifying potential alignments* as they do on diagnosing business situations and defining solutions. As someone who was used to managing operations over which she had a lot of control, Irina naturally focused on the "technical" side of learning. She sought to understand the business, identify key issues, and propose solutions. Her experience, and perhaps her temperament, didn't prepare her to focus on political learning. Your insights about how others' agendas do (and do not) align with your own can be an essential point of departure for effective corporate diplomacy. (Figure 3-1 provides a graphic summary of these alliances.)

FIGURE 3-1

Agendas, alliances, and relationships

This diagram of alliances points out the foundation for creating strong ones: understanding the differences between business alliances and business relationships. A critical factor is the presence (or absence) of shared long- or short-term agendas.

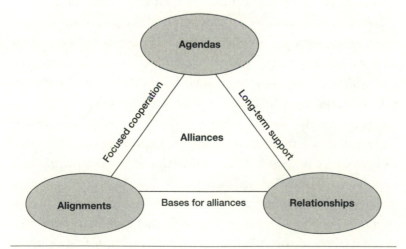

Defining Your Influence Objectives

When viewed through the lens of corporate diplomacy, Irina's challenge is a lot like that facing diplomats charged with negotiating a major treaty between, say, the United States and the European Union: the current status quo reflects a long-standing compromise between the two sides. It may be a flawed pact, but it's more or less stable—until something or someone comes along seeking to create a new and different equilibrium.

So besides knowing how and why to build alliances and relationships—and understanding the difference between the two—it's also essential for new leaders to be clear about their influence objectives: what do they hope to achieve?

Irina's goal should be to try to fashion a *grand bargain* between her new (direct) and old (indirect) bosses and their respective organizations over how important product formulation and packaging decisions will be made. The corporate marketing and R&D organizations will naturally favor more centralization. The managing directors in the EMEA region will jump at opportunities for more decentralization. An agreement, if it can be found at all, will consist of a package of trades that both sides can support.

To secure such an agreement, Irina will have to orchestrate and facilitate a complex set of synchronized negotiations—both between and within the two opposing sides. It's unlikely she'll be able to achieve complete unanimity because some people will have far too much invested in the status quo. So she should focus instead on winning a critical mass of support for agreement on both sides.

Had Irina understood this from the start, she might have focused her initial efforts differently—not just on diagnosing problems and proposing rational solutions but also on understanding how her agenda fit into the broader political landscape on both sides of the Atlantic. She would not have just assumed that the strength of her case would carry the day; nor would she have felt compelled to win over every single stakeholder. A better way to begin would have been for her to identify the specific alliances she needed to build and how she could leverage existing networks of influencers in the organization. This process of mapping the influence landscape also might have helped her identify any potential restraining forces: What or who might stand in the way of people moving in her direction? How could she get those in opposition to finally say yes?

Mapping the Influence Landscape

Armed with a deeper understanding of how alliances and relationships *really* work and the kinds of changes you'd eventually like to implement in the organization, you're ready for the next step: finding the chief influencers and determining what you need them to do and when you need them to do it. Figure 3-2 provides a simple tool for capturing this information. Additionally, it's often useful to summarize the results of such an analysis

FIGURE 3-2

Identifying influential players

Start to map your influence landscape by identifying influential players, what you need them to do, and when you need them to do it.

Who	What	When

FIGURE 3-3

Irina's influence map

This diagram summarizes relationships among key players in Irina's situation. She is effectively a mediator between the corporate and EMEA organizations.

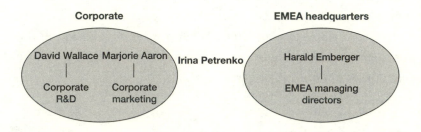

visually in an influence map, illustrated for Irina's situation in figure 3-3.

Winning and Blocking Alliances

A critical question to ask yourself is which players on either side of the situation are essential for building a *winning alliance*—a set of players who collectively have the influence necessary to shift the status quo.[1] Irina Petrenko, for instance, needs to secure agreement for her proposals from Marjorie Aaron and David Wallace on the corporate side and from Harald Emberger on the EMEA side. But it is likely that they will be influenced to a significant degree by the opinions of others in their respective organizations. To achieve her objective, Irina will have to build winning alliances within the corporate R&D and marketing groups as well as in the EMEA organization.

Conversely, it also pays to think hard about potential *blocking alliances*—those who seek to preserve the status quo and have the influence to do it. (After all, any significant change is likely to create winners *and* losers.) Which influencers might band together to try to block progress, and why? Are there particular influential individuals on each side who are likely to be opposed? How might they organize and seek to impede the process? If you have a good sense of where opposing groups might spring up, you can blunt their strategies—or even prevent them from coalescing in the first place.

Mapping Influence Networks

To gain insight into potential winning and blocking alliances, it helps to look for patterns of influence (both formal and informal) across an organization—specifically, who defers to whom on a given set of issues, particularly on the issues of concern to you. These *influence networks* can play a huge role in determining whether change ultimately happens or not. They exist because formal authority is by no means the only source of power in organizations, and because people tend to defer to others' opinions when it comes to important issues and decisions. Marjorie Aaron, for example, may defer to people in her organization with specific expertise on the impact of packaging changes on brand identity. The result is a set of channels for communication and persuasion that operate in parallel with the formal ones. Sometimes these informal channels support what the formal organization is trying to do; sometimes they subvert it.

There are several techniques new leaders can use to quickly gain more insight into these political dynamics. The first approach is to make some reasonable guesses about who the important players will be given the business issues you're confronting; arrange some meetings; and then listen—actively and attentively. Ask lots of questions, phrased in ways that won't trigger defensiveness. If you aren't satisfied with an answer, ask the question two or three different ways during the discussion. Propose what-if scenarios as a way to elicit thoughtful advice from the people with whom you're speaking.

The second strategy is to constantly scan for subtle signs of status and influence during meetings, hallway chats, and other interactions. Who speaks to whom about what? Who sits and stands where? Who defers to whom when certain topics are being discussed? When an issue is raised, where do people's eyes track?

Over time, the patterns of influence will become clearer, and you'll be able to identify those vital individuals who exert disproportionate influence because of their informal authority, expertise, or sheer force of personality. If you can convince these opinion leaders that your priorities and goals have merit, broader acceptance of your ideas is likely to follow. Additionally, you may be able to discern existing alliances—those groups of people who explicitly or implicitly band together to pursue specific goals or protect certain privileges. If these alliances support your agenda, you will gain leverage. If they oppose you, you may have no choice but to break them up or establish new ones.

Identifying Supporters, Opponents, and "Persuadables"

The work you've done to map influence networks in your organization can also help you to pinpoint potential supporters, opponents, and persuadables. Supporters could include anyone in the organization who shares your vision for the future, staffers who've been working for changes of their own, or other new leaders who haven't yet become part of the status quo.

Opponents are those who are most likely to resist what you hope to accomplish. They may disagree with you for any number of reasons: They disagree with your business case for change. They're comfortable with the status quo—perhaps *too* comfortable.

They're afraid the changes you're proposing will deprive them of power. They're afraid your agenda will negatively affect the people, processes, and cultural attributes they care about (the organization's traditional definitions of *value*, for instance). And finally, they're afraid of seeming or feeling incompetent if they have trouble adapting to the changes you're proposing. If you understand your opponents' reasons for railing against your initiatives, you'll be better equipped to counter their arguments—and perhaps even turn them into supporters.

And speaking of conversions, don't forget about the persuadables—those people in the organization who are indifferent to or undecided about your plans but who might be persuaded to throw their support your way if you can figure out where your mutual interests intersect.

An influence network diagram can help to summarize what you learn about these influential constituencies. Irina's assessment of the patterns of influence at Van Lear Foods is summarized in figure 3-4.

As the center circle of the exhibit suggests, the critical decision makers at Van Lear—at least as it pertains to the issues Irina cares about—are two major players from the corporate arena, Marjorie Aaron and David Wallace, and the head of EMEA operations, Harald Emberger. Irina needs all three to agree with her change initiatives, so they jointly constitute a winning alliance.

But, as the arrows in the diagram indicate, these principal decision makers will also be influenced by people within their own organizations. (Wider arrows denote a greater degree of influence.) Marjorie Aaron will be strongly influenced by Eric McNulty, her vice president of marketing strategy, and Tim Marshall, a vice president in the corporate strategy group. David Wallace will be influenced by Catherine Clark, his vice president of new-product-development planning, and Tim Marshall. Harald Emberger will

FIGURE 3-4

Influence networks at Van Lear Foods

This diagram illustrates the key influence relationships that will shape decision making on the issues Irina Petrenko is trying to address in her organization.

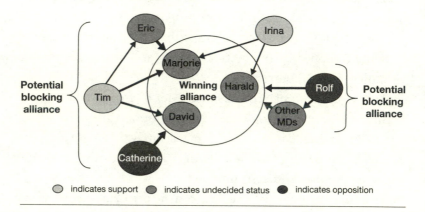

be influenced by the collective opinions of the country managers who report to him. But Rolf Eiklid, the longtime managing director of the Nordic countries, will be influential both in shaping Harald's views and in influencing the other managing directors. The diagram also shows that Irina herself has significant influence on Harald and some on Marjorie.

The players' support or opposition is indicated in the diagram —the darkest screen means opposition, light gray means support, and medium gray means undecided. According to the chart, Catherine is opposed to Irina's proposals to shift the balance in centralization and decentralization of key decisions, Tim is in favor of changes, and Eric is undecided. Given that David is heavily influenced by Catherine, and Marjorie is moderately influenced by Eric, Catherine and Eric form a potential blocking alliance on the corporate side. Moreover, if the country managers side with Rolf, who is also opposed to Irina's proposed changes, they could form a blocking alliance on the EMEA side. Note that, once again, she has to win a critical mass of support on both sides for overall agreement to occur.

Developing an Influence Strategy

Now that you've conducted a thorough analysis of the influence patterns in your organization, identified crucial players and alliances, and mapped out potential scenarios, it's time to devise a strategy for leading through influence rather than authority—a critical factor of succeeding in your new role and creating the momentum for change.

The first step is to understand how key players perceive their *interests*. Interests are what they care about. Key here is to understand what potential opponents like Rolf and Catherine are opposed to and why. Are there specific losses that could be avoided? Is there something they can be given—a valuable trade—that might help compensate? Now do the same analysis for potential supporters. What might they find attractive about what you are proposing? What concerns might they have that you could address up front?

Understanding people's perceptions of their interests is only half the story, however. The other half is to understand how they perceive their *alternatives*. What are the options from which people believe they can choose? Critical here is to assess whether opponents like Catherine believe that resistance—overt or covert— can succeed in preserving the status quo. If so, then you have to find ways to reshape perceptions of alternatives so that sustaining the status quo is no longer a viable option. Once people perceive that some change is going to happen, the game shifts from outright opposition to a competition to influence what sort of change will occur. The implication for Irina is that she must convince the key decision makers—Marjorie, David, and Harald— that the current situation is not acceptable, that some change must take place. Figure 3-5 provides a simple tool for capturing this information.

Armed with your assessment of interests and alternatives, you can think about how you will frame your argument. This means thinking through the rationale and data in support of your goals. It's well worth the time to get the framing right. Indeed, if Irina can't develop and communicate a compelling business case in support of her proposed changes, nothing else she does will have much impact. Your messages should take an appropriate tone, resonate with the interests of influential players, and, critically, shape how they see their options. Irina should, for example, explore what it would take to move Rolf from being opposed to at least being neutral and, ideally, supportive. Does he have specific concerns that she can address? Is there a set of trades that he would find attractive if implementation could be guaranteed? Are

FIGURE 3-5

Analyzing interests and alternatives

Use this table to assess how influential players are likely to perceive their interests (what they care about) and their alternatives (what choices they believe they have).

Who	Interests	Alternatives

there ways of helping him advance other agendas he cares about in exchange for his support of Irina's ideas?

Once you have thought through the framing, consider using the following techniques for creating the momentum for change: *incrementalism, sequencing,* and *shuttle and summit diplomacy.* All three work by shifting how key players perceive their alternatives.

Incrementalism. This approach involves moving people in desired directions in small steps and turning minor commitments into major ones over time. It is highly effective because each small step taken creates a new psychological reference point for deciding whether to take the next one. For instance, Irina could invite people to meet—initially just to explore the centralization-versus-flexibility "problem." Over time, however, the group could analyze each of the issues involved. And finally, after they have deliberately walked through all major concerns, the participants could discuss some basic principles for what a good solution might look like.

Sequencing. This technique involves intentionally structuring the order and the way in which you approach various influencers in the organization.[2] If you approach the right people first, you can set in motion a virtuous cycle of alliance building. Once you gain one respected ally, you will find it easier to recruit others—and your resource base will increase exponentially. With broader support, the likelihood increases that your agenda will succeed, making it easier still to recruit more supporters. Based on her assessment of patterns of influence at Van Lear, Irina should definitely meet first with corporate strategy VP Tim Marshall to solidify his support and arm him with additional information for persuading the likes of Marjorie, David, and Eric on the corporate side. Irina should meet with Eric second—after Tim has had a chance to bend the undecided executive's ear.

Shuttle and summit diplomacy. This strategy involves convening combinations of one-on-one and group meetings to create the momentum for change. The critical point here is getting the mix right. One-on-one meetings are effective for getting the lay of the land—for instance, hearing people's positions, shaping their views by providing new or extra information, or potentially negotiating side deals. But the participants in a serious negotiation often won't be willing to make their final concessions and commitments unless they are sitting face-to-face with others—which is when summit meetings are particularly effective. A note of caution, however: if the process isn't ripe—that is, if people haven't had enough time to understand that they need to make concessions—such summit meetings can pave the way for blocking alliances to form or prompt players with veto power to withdraw from the room.

Ultimately Irina was unsuccessful in achieving the desired shifts in decision making. By the time she shifted her focus away from problem solving and toward political management, too much polarization had occurred. Seeing that the gap between the EMEA and headquarters had become unbridgeable, she wisely retreated and focused on working effectively within the existing framework. While disappointing, this was not fatal, and she learned a host of valuable lessons that made her much more effective in dealing with other cross-organizational challenges.

Corporate Diplomacy Checklist

1. What are the critical alliances you need to build—both within your organization and externally—to advance your agenda?

2. What agendas are other key players in the organization pursuing? Where might they align with yours and where might they come into conflict?

3. What relationships could form the basis for long-term, broad-based alliances? Where might you be able to leverage shorter-term agreements to pursue specific objectives?

4. How does influence operate in the organization? Who defers to whom on key issues of concern?

5. Who is likely to support your agenda? Who is likely to oppose you? Who is persuadable? What are their interests and alternatives?

6. What are the elements of an effective influence strategy? How should you frame your arguments? Might dynamic influence tools such as incrementalism and sequencing help?

4 The Onboarding Challenge

THE MANDATE DAVID JONES HAD BEEN GIVEN SEEMED CLEAR enough: Bring some discipline and focus to a relatively young and fast-growing company that designed and manufactured wind turbines. But just a few months into his new job as COO of Energix, David was wondering if he'd been set up to fail.

It had seemed like the perfect opportunity for an ambitious executive with such strong leadership skills. After majoring in finance in college, David had joined an iconic *Fortune* 100 manufacturing firm that was both global and diversified. First in the supply chain unit, and later in R&D, David had risen steadily through the ranks to become vice president of new-product development for the company's electrical distribution division.

David learned to lead in a company that was renowned for its management "bench strength" and its commitment to talent development. The culture leaned somewhat toward a command-and-control style of leadership, but people were still expected to speak their minds—and did. The company used state-of-the-art measurement systems to relentlessly weed out underperformers, but its reputation as a leadership factory made it relatively easy for the firm to recruit fresh talent. When the company needed to fill senior-level positions, it rarely hired from the outside. It didn't have to.

The company had long been a leader in the adoption and refinement of the top management methodologies, including Total Quality Management, Lean Manufacturing, and Six Sigma. In fact, virtually everyone in the company had been trained in some elements of the latter; David was a black belt in Six Sigma. The result was an organization where people truly believed that "you can't manage what you don't measure." They had internalized process management as though it were religion.

David's superb quantitative skills and natural aptitude for systems thinking were important factors in his rapid ascent through the ranks—those and the aggressive nature he had honed as a linebacker for his high school and college football teams. He loved nothing more than tackling a problem and wrestling it to the ground. At well over six feet tall, David intimidated some. At the same time, he had been able to engender a strong sense of loyalty among his people because of the intensity with which he upheld the company's commitment to leadership development.

Needless to say, the manufacturing company was fertile ground for corporate recruiters: personnel decisions tended to be of the "up or out" variety, and typically there was a surplus of good candidates for relatively few senior jobs. So, like most executives at the firm, David got calls from headhunters regularly. Sometimes he listened to their pitches; it couldn't hurt to gauge his value in the outside job market, right? But he'd never really been tempted—until the opportunity to become chief operating officer of Energix came along.

Just six years old, Energix had been funded by Silicon Valley venture capitalists before going public. Capitalizing on increasing energy prices, Energix had established a strong and fast-growing position in wind turbine design and manufacturing.

The company was doing well; it had weathered the typical start-up transitions of going from two people to twenty to two hundred to two thousand and was now poised to become a major corporation. As a result, the CEO had told David more than once during recruitment and his final round of interviews that things had to change. "We need to become more disciplined," the chief executive had said. "We've succeeded by staying focused and working as a team. We know each other, we trust each other, and we've come a long way together. But we need to be more systematic in how we do things, or we won't be able to capitalize on and sustain our new size."

The decision to appoint a COO was itself a big step for Energix. The CEO had never appointed a number two executive before. Previously he had relied on tight working relationships with the CFO and the heads of R&D and operations, all of whom were members of the company's founding team. With the company's growth, though, had come more internal tensions—and at a time when the CEO needed to focus more of his time on external relationships.

David liked the COO opportunity—quite a bit. On the surface, it appeared to be a near-perfect match for his skills. He would be offered an attractive compensation package linked to the company's growth. He would have overall responsibility for internal operations, with broad scope to define his agenda. He understood that his first major task would be to identify, systematize, and improve the core processes of the organization—essentially laying the foundation for sustained growth for the company.

So David took the plunge and joined Energix, digging into the new job with his usual gusto. In the weeks before he formally took the role, he absorbed every piece of data he could about the company and its operations. He also conducted in-depth fact-finding interviews with all the members of Energix's senior management committee (SMC) and other key people in new-product development, operations, and finance.

What emerged was a portrait of a company that had been run largely by the seat of its collective pants. Many important operational and financial processes were not well established; others weren't sufficiently controlled. In new-product development alone, there were dozens of projects with inadequate specifications or insufficiently precise milestones and deliverables. The good news was that one critical project, Energix's next-generation large turbine, was probably going to market in the next few months, but it was nearly a year behind schedule and way over budget. David came away from his fact-finding exercise wondering just what or who had held Energix together—and feeling more convinced than ever that he could push this company to the next level.

The problems began soon after David's formal appointment. The SMC meetings started out frustrating and just got worse. The committee had decided that the CEO would continue to chair these meetings—just until David got established, they said. For his part, David, who was used to a high level of discipline in meetings, with clear agendas and actionable decisions made in tight time frames, found the committee members' elliptical discussions and consensus-driven process agonizing. Particularly troubling to him was the lack of open discussion about pressing issues and the sense that commitments were being made through back channels. When David raised a sensitive or provocative issue with the SMC, or pressed others in the room for commitments to act, the committee members would either fall silent or recite a litany of reasons why things couldn't be done a certain way. David approached the CEO with his concerns and was told it would probably just take more time for him to understand "the way we do things here."

Two months in, with his patience frayed, David decided to simply focus on what he had been hired to do: revamp the processes to support the company's growth. New-product development was his first target, for several reasons: his fact finding had pointed out numerous holes in that function, which touched many other parts of the company, and given his previous experience, R&D was something David understood quite well. So he convened a meeting of the heads of R&D, operations, and finance to discuss how to proceed. At that gathering, David presented a plan for setting up teams that would map out existing processes and conduct a thorough redesign effort. He also outlined the required resource commitments—for instance, assigning some strong people from R&D, operations, and finance to participate in the teams and hiring external consultants to support the analysis.

Given the conversations he'd had with the CEO during the recruiting process and the clear mandate he felt he'd been given, David was shocked by the stonewalling he encountered in the meeting. The attendees listened attentively but wouldn't commit themselves or their people to David's plan. Instead, they urged David to bring his plan before the whole SMC since it affected so many parts of the company and had the potential to be disruptive if not managed carefully. (He later learned that two of the participants had gone to the CEO soon after the meeting to register their concerns; David was "a bull in a china shop," according to one. "We have to be careful not to upset some delicate balances as we get out the next-gen turbine," said another. And both were of the firm opinion that "letting 'Jones' run things might not be the right way to go.")

Even more troubling, as David tried to implement his ideas, he experienced a noticeable and worrisome chill in his relationship with the CEO. Previously, the CEO had reached out to him frequently. But increasingly, the onus was on David to initiate conversations. Their discussions had become both more formal and more formulaic, as the CEO increasingly stressed the importance of the launch of the next-generation turbine—indirectly suggesting that the product rollout should take precedence over efforts to improve processes. The CEO also deflected discussions about when David would begin to run his own internal operational meetings.

The Onboarding Challenge

As David Jones's story suggests, joining an established business from the outside is never easy—the new leadership role is often ill defined, the organizational architecture will most likely be unfamiliar, and the politics are even more complex than usual. But such transitions are becoming increasingly common: because of their inabilities to build their own deep benches of talent, and given their ever-present mandates for global growth, more and more companies are looking outside for senior-level executives and then seeking effective ways to "onboard" them.

It follows, then, that firms that have spent a great deal of time and money to identify and recruit talent can ill afford for their newly hired executives to underperform or, even worse, become so frustrated that they decide to leave before they get a chance to gain traction. That's where successful onboarding comes in. If new leaders are welcomed into a supportive environment—one that encourages them to realize personal and organizational aspirations—they'll produce much more quickly and are more likely to stay around for a while.

But while the onboarding challenge is receiving more attention these days, many talented leaders still don't believe their companies do a good job transitioning newly hired executives. A recent survey of senior HR executives I conducted through the IMD Business School in Lausanne, Switzerland, revealed that 54 percent of the respondents thought their companies did an inadequate job of executive onboarding.[1]

It's also important to note that the onboarding challenge applies not just in those instances when new leaders are transitioning between two different companies, as David Jones was, but also when he or she is moving between units of a company. In fact, my studies have shown that on average, *moves between units in the same company are rated to be 70 percent as difficult as joining a new company.* The primary reason is that units of the same company often have very different subcultures, the result of "bolt-on" acquisitions or the nature of work done within the unit.

Organizational Immunology

To increase their odds of success in their new roles, onboarding executives need to recognize that each company has its own distinct "immune system," comprising the organization's culture and political networks. Just as the function of the human immune system is to protect the body from foreign organisms, so is the organizational immune system ready to isolate and destroy outsiders who seek to introduce "bad" ideas.

To protect the human body, the immune system must demonstrate equal parts under- and over-reactivity. If it responds too weakly to warning signals, it may fail to mount an effective attack against a virus or may permit a damaged cell to grow into a cancerous tumor. But if the system overreacts, it will go after good things in the body, producing autoimmune conditions such as rheumatoid arthritis or multiple sclerosis.

Similarly, when the culture and political networks in organizations are working well, they prevent "bad thinking" and "bad people" from entering the building and doing damage. If the company's immune system responds weakly to warning signs, bad leadership can infect the business and do tremendous damage. But if the system is working *too* well, even potentially good things coming from the outside can be destroyed. Specifically, the organizational system isolates and weakens the disruptive "agent"—in this case, David Jones—until he or she decides to leave. Even much-needed agents of change can succumb. In one Silicon Valley technology company I looked at, the success rate for outside hires was close to zero. And in a leading financial services firm I worked with, the gallows humor was, "When a new person is hired from the outside, a bullet gets fired at his head. The question is whether he can dodge it in time."

It's critical for transitioning executives to assume their new roles in ways that won't trigger attacks from their organizations' immune systems. Key is not to do things that cause you to be labeled as "dangerous."

Thinking you have all the answers. David came in to Energix convinced that weak processes were the core problem and that he had the skills and knowledge to fix it. It was easy for him to reach this conclusion because process improvement was one of his core strengths, and he naturally interpreted the CEO's description of the company's need for "discipline" through this lens. He likewise viewed available data about the company in this light. So he came in expecting that everyone understood that this was "the problem" and agreed that he was there to fix it. Even if he was right, *it didn't matter*. His naturally aggressive approach to leading change inevitably offended influential people, initiating an immunological reaction at Energix.

Wanting to bring in your own people. Think hard before you reflexively reach back to your old organization for talent, lest it contribute to triggering an immune reaction. (David didn't fall into this trap, although he did try to bring in consultants that he formerly had worked with.) It is especially risky to "bring in your own people" if your new organization is a realignment or sustaining-success situation. If you are leading a turnaround and need to assemble a team quickly, it can make sense to hire capable people you know and trust. But in less-urgent situations, the reflex to bring in people you know can easily be interpreted to mean you're dissatisfied with the level of talent in your new organization. If you need to replace people on your team, the first place to look is one level below. The second best option is to hire people from the outside—*just not from your old organization(s)*. Once you've built up some credibility and trust in the new organization, it's often all right to call previous colleagues—but beware of moving too quickly when hiring for critical positions.

Creating the impression that "there is no good here." This is a related syndrome that can take hold during the early days of your transition, as you're looking at the data and learning more about your new company. There is a natural tendency to focus on the problems—identifying them, prioritizing them, and drafting plans to fix them. But you can't talk only about the problems you've observed and not about the organization's strengths and accomplishments. It's not enough that *you* recognize the positives; you have to demonstrate to others in the organization that you truly value these attributes. If you create the impression that you believe "there is no good here," the organizational immune system will certainly kick in.

Ignoring the need to learn and adapt. Finally, a sure way to generate an immune attack is to behave in ways that are obviously countercultural and, critically, show little commitment to learning and adapting. Early on, you're bound to act in ways that are culturally inconsistent, simply because you're new to the environment. Usually, you'll be forgiven for this. The danger comes when people think you have what political columnist George Will once described as "a learning curve as flat as Kansas." David Jones, for instance, recognized that decisions were made differently at Energix than they were at his old company. But instead of trying to understand the culture, adapt to it, and eventually shape it, he got frustrated and tried to launch a frontal assault early on. The system, of course, wouldn't allow it.

Indeed, once they're activated, organizational immune systems are tough to beat—which is why you must build up tolerances instead, convincing the organization that you belong there even as you seek to make difficult changes. To do this, you'll need to focus on three critical tasks very early in your tenure: adapting to the culture, making political connections, and aligning expectations.

Adapting to the Culture

Perhaps the most daunting challenge for transitioning executives is adapting to the unfamiliar cultures in their new companies or units. The first and most important step, then, is to understand what the culture is, at a macro level, and how it's manifested in the particular organization or unit you're joining. In doing this it

FIGURE 4-1

Layers of culture

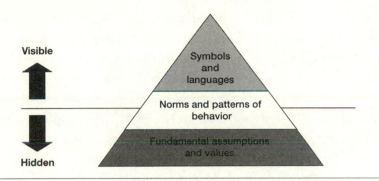

helps to think of yourself as an anthropologist sent to study a newly discovered culture.

So what is culture? It's a set of consistent patterns people follow for communicating, thinking, and acting, all grounded in their shared assumptions and values. The culture in any company will generally be multilayered, as illustrated in figure 4-1.[2]

At the top of the pyramid are the surface elements of culture—the symbols, shared languages, and other things most visible to outsiders. Obvious symbols might include how people dress, how the office space is organized, how perks are distributed within certain work groups. Likewise, every organization typically has a shared language—a long list of acronyms, for instance, describing business units, products, processes, projects, and other elements of the company. At this level, it is relatively easy for newcomers to figure out how to fit in. If people at your level don't wear plaid, then you shouldn't either. If your peers and subordinates are accustomed to receiving certain perks, then it's probably best for you, as a new leader, to adopt and maintain those benefits. And it's essential that you invest in learning to speak the local patois early and completely—unless, of course, you're intentionally trying to signal some sort of culture-change process.

Beneath the surface layer of symbols and language lies a deeper, less visible set of organizational norms and accepted patterns of behavior. These elements of culture include things like how people get support for important initiatives, how they win recognition for their accomplishments, and how they view meetings—are they seen as forums for discussion or rubber-stamp sessions? (See the box "Identifying Cultural Norms.") These companywide norms and patterns are difficult to discern, and often become evident only after one has spent some time in a new environment—something David Jones should have acknowledged. He had learned to lead in a culture where everyone accepted the importance of having and following solid processes to get things done. But the culture at Energix was much more centered on relationships, a function of its status as a relatively young start-up. Even if it really was essential for him to focus the company on more and better processes, it was dangerous for him to assume from day one that the existing emphasis on relationships as a means for getting things done was dysfunctional—and to openly challenge such a crucial element of the culture.

And finally, underlying all corporate cultures are the fundamental assumptions that everyone in the company has about "the way the world works"—the shared values that infuse and reinforce all the other elements in the pyramid. A good example is the general beliefs people in the company have about the "right" way to distribute power based on position. Are executives in particular roles given lots of decision-making power from day one, or is the degree of authority a function of seniority? Or does the organization operate according to consensus, where the ability to persuade is key? Again, these elements of the culture are largely hidden from view and usually become clear only after you've spent time in the environment.

Identifying Cultural Norms

The following domains are areas in which cultural norms may vary significantly from company to company. Transitioning leaders should use this checklist to help them figure out how things *really* work in the organizations they're joining.

- *Influence.* How do people get support for critical initiatives? Is it more important to have the support of a "patron" within the senior team, or affirmation from your peers and direct reports that your idea is a good one?

- *Meetings.* Are meetings filled with dialogue on hard issues, or are they simply forums for publicly ratifying agreements that have been reached in private?

- *Execution.* When it comes time to get things done, which matters more: a deep understanding of processes, or knowing the right people?

- *Conflict.* Can people talk openly about difficult issues without fear of retribution? Or do they avoid conflict—or, even worse, push it to lower levels where it can wreak havoc?

- *Recognition.* Does the company promote "stars," rewarding those who very visibly and vocally drive business initiatives? Or does it encourage team players, rewarding those who lead authoritatively but quietly and collaboratively?

- *Ends versus means.* Are there any restrictions on how you achieve results? Does the organization have a well-defined, well-communicated set of values that is reinforced through positive and negative incentives?

Once you have this "macro" understanding of the discrete elements of corporate culture, you can more easily determine what kind of corporate culture you're stepping into and how it's different from others you've experienced. This process needs to start early: you should be asking culture questions as part of the interview process, using the checklist to help formulate your queries. Be careful not to take everything you hear as gospel, however. Both sides will still be in the courtship phase, after all, and hiring executives understandably might be a little reluctant to pull back the curtain on the organization completely. If possible, try to schedule some chats with people who've left the company—on good terms and bad.

Once you're inside the building, you'll need to continue learning and adapting as quickly as possible. Inevitably, you'll commit some "boundary violations," acting in ways that aren't consistent with mainstream behaviors. You can't expect to fit in right away, and, in most companies, people won't expect you to. But they will expect you to *recognize* your faux pas, do the appropriate things to *recover*, and *recalibrate* your behavior accordingly.

Clearly, then, it's critical to familiarize yourself with the recognize-recover-recalibrate (R3) loop and work through each stage as quickly and efficiently as possible. Good resources in this regard are "cultural interpreters" in your new organization or unit. These are typically long-timers at the company who exemplify the culture but can also be reflective about it and, ultimately, provide useful guidance to the transitioning executive. (The same resources can and should be sought out when making international moves, as I discuss in chapter 5.) Finding all these traits in one individual can be difficult. But the search will be well worth it: these interpreters can be invaluable resources in helping you to recognize when you've overstepped cultural bounds, to make appropriate amends, and to reset expectations (your own and the company's).

As you learn more about the culture, you'll also need to consider the degree of adaptation versus change that will be necessary. The ratio will vary depending on where the company is in its life cycle and the particular business challenge it faces. (In chapters 6, 7, and 8, I talk more about the STARS framework that transitioning leaders can use to determine the context they're operating in.) If you're entering a turnaround situation, for instance, wholesale change will probably be on your agenda—including a fundamental reworking of the corporate culture. In these instances, the organizational immune system is already weakened, and new ideas are typically welcome. Harder, though, are realignment situations, where the changes may be more incremental—and where a dysfunctional culture can often be a significant part of the problem. In these instances, resistance to change will obviously be much greater.

Making Political Connections

As David Jones learned, a bit harshly it seems, it's nearly impossible for onboarding executives to create any kind of momentum for organizational change when they aren't plugged into the company's political system—who has influence, who doesn't, which relationships are most critical, and so on. The second imperative for transitioning leaders, then, is to identify key stakeholders and begin to forge productive working relationships with them. Here, too, there are two traps to avoid: focusing on vertical relationships and mistaking titles for authority.

Looking only "up and down." There is a natural but dangerous tendency for onboarding leaders to focus too much on building vertical relationships early in their tenures—looking up to their bosses, down to their teams. As a result, the transitioning executives often neglect the lateral relationships they should be building and strengthening with peers, customers, and other outside constituencies. Looking back at David Jones's situation, for instance, he put far more emphasis on data collection and analysis than on getting to know people. So he didn't begin to build trust and credibility with key stakeholders. In his early meetings with the senior management committee, had he focused more on understanding the members, what they cared about, and how things worked in the organization, he would have been much less likely to provoke defensive reactions.

Mistaking titles for authority. When you're identifying the power players in your new company or unit, it's easy to turn to the usual suspects—large stakeholders, your new boss, some of your peers, and your direct reports. Those aren't the only true influencers, however: every company has an informal or "shadow" organization as well as a formal one.[3] There are always some well-placed, highly respected managers in the organization whose influence far exceeds their formal authority.

Keeping this pair of pitfalls in mind, the best way for onboarding managers to stockpile precious relationship capital is to act deliberately—targeting the right people, assessing those individuals' agendas and alignments, and forging connections based on common interests. When it comes to identifying key players, it's probably best to radiate out, carefully working through a comprehensive list of parties in the unit, in the company, in the larger organization, in the partnership community, in the analyst community, and so forth. (See the box "The Stakeholder Checklist" for a rundown of potential targets for your attention.) Your new boss may be able to help you narrow the field, as can a representative from HR.

Once you've figured out the "who" side of the equation, you'll need to focus on the "what." What agendas are key stakeholders

The Stakeholder Checklist

As you transition into a new business unit or company, you'll need to identify those people inside and outside the organization who can help you push your agenda forward. Here's a list of the potential candidates you might reach out to.

In Your Organization

- *Boss(es).* What are their key expectations? What can you do to help them get some wins? If you have more than one boss, where do their interests line up, and where are they potentially in conflict?

- *Peers.* Who most and least needs your help to realize their goals? Who most and least affects your ability to realize your goals? Where will you most need to expend political capital to gain support for your proposed initiatives?

- *Direct reports.* Which of your new direct reports has historically wielded the most influence on important decisions (it may vary from issue to issue), and why? Who is likely to support, oppose, or be indifferent to your proposed initiatives? How are existing alliances within the team arranged?

- *Other employees.* Who wields the most informal influence in your organization, and why? Which of these shadow influencers is likely to support, oppose, or be indifferent to your proposed initiatives?

In the Larger Company

- *Corporate.* If you are operating in a unit that is part of a larger corporate structure, who most influences your ability to get things done by providing financial approvals and access to talent and other resources, and by defining the legal and regulatory boundaries?

- *Internal customers.* Which internal customers most influence the performance of your unit? What do they care most about? How can you help them solve problems that are important to them?

- *Internal suppliers.* Which internal suppliers most influence the performance of your unit? What do they care most about? How can you help them solve problems that are important to them?

Outside the Company

- *Customers.* Which external customers most influence the performance of your organization? What do they care most about? How can you help them solve problems that are important to them?

- *Suppliers.* Which external suppliers most influence the performance of your organization? What do they care most about? How can you help them solve problems that are important to them?

- *Rule makers.* Who in government or the nonprofit sector has the greatest ability to significantly change "the rules of the game" for your organization? What do these players care most about? How can you judiciously build bridges with them?

- *Analysts and the media.* Based on their observations and interpretations of your company's performance, who in the analyst community and the media have the most influence with investors and the public? What do those institutional groups care most about? How can you judiciously build bridges with them?

most interested in pursuing? How do their interests line up with your own, and where are they in conflict? Why are these stakeholders pursuing these agendas? When do irreversible business decisions absolutely, positively have to be made—where are the key decision points, milestones, and other action-forcing events?

As a transitioning leader, you enter the organization with a zero balance in your relationship account. As discussed in chapter 3 on corporate diplomacy, you can build up that account quickly by understanding where others are coming from—and, when possible, helping them advance those agenda items that are good for both the organization and the individual.

Aligning Expectations

David Jones was positive he understood the mandate from Energix's CEO—bring structure to a firm that had long conducted business on the fly. More process, less improvisation. But the COO's interpretation of the organizational-change challenge didn't quite match the goals and expectations of others on the senior team. Which, of course, points out the importance of the third imperative for onboarding executives: ensure that you understand what the expectations for success are and that you can accept those goals. Otherwise, you, like David, can fall into the following transition traps.

Failing to check, and recheck. The expectations that David and his new boss negotiated during the recruitment process weren't necessarily the ones others in the company agreed to. How is that possible? *Because recruiting is like romance, and employment is like marriage:* during the recruiting period, neither party gets a complete view of the other. Both the leader and the organization put on their best possible faces, not necessarily to deceive but to accentuate the positive. So the organization may come away with inflated expectations of what the new hire can accomplish, and the new hire may think he or she has more authority to make changes than really exists. As a result, someone like David comes in, confident in his mandate, acts on his beliefs—and generates a predictable backlash.

Missing unspoken expectations. Some people simply are better communicators than others; this applies to bosses as much as it does to spouses, customers, business partners, or any other counterpart. The CEO of Energix wasn't articulate enough, it seems. He left out some important elements that impacted David's mandate—for example, that the real first priority was to successfully launch the next-generation turbine. It's therefore essential for the onboarding leader to tease out *all* of the new boss's aspirations and goals for the unit or company. Triangulation can be a useful technique for doing this: ask your boss the same question in three somewhat different ways, and see whether the answers vary. Testing comprehension can be another good tactic: during important conversations about expectations, summarize and share your understanding of critical takeaways from the discussion. You can do this verbally, as the session draws to a close, or in writing, in a follow-up e-mail.

Lack of agreement on the business challenge at hand. If you think parts of the organization need a significant overhaul but your boss thinks incremental improvements are in order—or vice versa—you're in trouble. When views about the most important challenges facing the unit or company are dramatically different, it's important for you to step back and take the time to educate all key constituencies about the situation; don't commit to any specific goals until all parties can get closer to agreement.

Negotiating expectations and resources separately. Onboarding leaders often get into trouble by negotiating expectations and resources sequentially and not simultaneously. Usually this happens when the transitioning executive is pressed to make commitments before he or she really understands what it will take to meet them. If you're in such a situation, it's important to try to judiciously defer decisions until you're further along the learning curve. It's not always possible to do this. You can, however, try to negotiate the process of engagement early on—making it clear that you'd like time to diagnose the situation, present an assessment and plan, and then revisit expectations and time lines.

To avert these traps, transitioning leaders need to have five important conversations with their new bosses concerning leadership style, the business situation, expectations for success, resource allocation, and course correction—with the talks happening roughly in that order. (See "The Five Conversations.")

The Five Conversations

Below is a list of five conversations transitioning leaders should have with their bosses along with guiding questions that can help both sides come to some agreement about the organizational-change challenge the new leader has been brought in to tackle.

- *The style conversation*
  - How can we best work together?
  - How do you prefer me to communicate with you?
  - What level of detail do you want concerning my organization or unit and the issues I'm confronting?
  - How do you prefer to make decisions?

- *The situation conversation*
  - How do you see the STARS situation in my organization as a whole? In important subcomponents?
  - On what do you base these assessments?
  - What's your level of certainty?
- *The expectations conversation*
  - What am I expected to accomplish, and in what time frame?
  - What would constitute "early wins" for you?
  - What outcomes do I most need to avoid?
- *The resources conversation*
  - What financial and other resources are available to me?
  - What scope do I have to make changes in my team?
  - To what extent will you visibly support me in making the case for change?
- *The course-adjustment conversation* (this typically should begin not later than the ninety-day mark)
  - How are things going so far?
  - What am I doing well?
  - Do you have areas of concern?

Creating Onboarding Systems

The onus is on the transitioning executive to become cognizant of her new company's or unit's culture, develop the right political connections, and negotiate the correct mandates. But there is much that companies can do to help accelerate these processes for the onboarding leader.

Accelerate cultural adaptation. HR and talent-management experts can provide a range of resources and programs for newly hired executives. Some are very easy to create and implement, such as providing an updated list of important terms and acronyms used in the company. Others are more difficult to deploy but can pack a powerful punch, such as giving newly hired leaders early insight into the organization's norms and values.

To do the latter, the company's hiring managers and the senior team have to be open about the culture, and willing and able to describe it and discuss it in great detail. Of course, some organizations don't like opening up about their cultures for fear that they'll scare away talented recruits who don't consider themselves a match. Better to be up front, however, lest new hires claim a bait-and-switch: they think they'll be operating in a certain culture and in fact are dealing with a completely different one.

Given a willingness to be open, the company can use a variety of means to capture and describe the culture for new leaders. For instance, I worked with one leading diversified health care company to research and write a compact account of the history and culture. This proved to be an invaluable resource to transitioning executives. In other situations I have created compilations of short video interviews with successful "onboarding survivors." These leaders, who've been there and done that, can obviously impart critical insights to newly hired executives. Companies can also assign a "cultural interpreter" to the onboarding manager; that way, she'll have a go-to resource for questions and insights about the corporate culture.

Accelerate the development of political connections. In effective onboarding processes, companies identify the full set of critical stakeholders and engage them before the executive formally joins the organization. Typically, a point person from HR touches base with the new hire's boss, peers, and direct reports to create this list. This point person also may encourage and support the transitioning executive in setting up and conducting early meetings with these stakeholders. New leader assimilation sessions and other structured assessment tools and programs can play an important role in speeding up relationship formation as well.

If the dedicated resources aren't available to support the process just described—for example, in a smaller company with less staff to assign to onboarding people—HR can instead provide hiring managers with a template to create a top 10 list of people with whom the transitioning leader should connect early on, as well as a template for drafting introductory e-mails to those people. Companies can also give transitioning executives tools, such as the influence mapping methodology discussed in chapter 3, to help them diagnose informal organizational networks, identify key alliances, and draft a plan for gaining support and creating momentum.

Accelerate expectations alignment. The company should make explicit the importance of structured discussions about expectations. These conversations should be a standard piece of the onboarding program, and there needs to be a clear process by which hiring managers and new leaders can negotiate expectations and resources. Some companies rely on the same systems they use for business planning. While helpful, these systems often need to be augmented with significant additional dialogue to ensure that alignment happens up, down, and sideways.

Aside from helping transitioning executives succeed in the three critical areas of culture, alliances, and expected outcomes, companies must also provide transition support in real time. Too much information early on can overwhelm, but waiting too long to impart critical data can create post-transition regret: "Why are you telling me this now, when I've already made mistakes?" In those first few days and months, onboarding executives will need a rolling supply of information from reliable resources who are willing to remain on standby for questions.

And finally, there must be a coherent relationship between the recruiting process and the onboarding process. Put another way, *the best transition support systems can't compensate for the sins of poor recruiting*—and there are far too many organizations out there that focus on bringing "stars" rather than "role players" into the fold, failing to consider whether those people are actually the best fit for the organization. An executive might have the "right" knowledge and experience but not the leadership style or values to match the company's culture. This certainly appears to have been at the root of David Jones's problems at Energix.

Companies that want to integrate their recruiting and onboarding processes must move beyond the standard linear process of job specification, interviewing, and hiring (see figure 4-2). They'll need to assess the risks and trade-offs of hiring internally versus externally given the business situation. If the company requires a complete turnaround, for example, it's less risky to hire from the outside than it would be in the case of a realignment. Why?

FIGURE 4-2

Integrating recruiting and onboarding

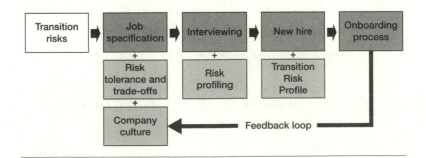

Because people in the organization are more likely to be open to, and perhaps even close to desperate for, outside perspectives.

Hiring managers also need to think through their tolerance for risk and the associated trade-offs between capability and fit. As the interviewing process proceeds, they can develop a Transition Risk Profile (available at www.YourNextMove.net) for the onboarding executive that identifies specific areas of support needed to reduce the risk of generating fatal reactions from the organizational immune system. Finally, note that the onboarding process can generate insight into company culture; this should be fed back to the system to inform recruiting in the future.

Onboarding Checklist

1. How can you accelerate your learning about the history and culture of your new organization? Are there cultural interpreters who can help you understand the nuances?

2. What do you need to do to strike the right balance between adapting to the culture versus trying to alter it? How can you avoid triggering a dangerous immune system attack?

3. Who are the stakeholders—within your new organization and externally—who will have significant influence over whether you can move your agenda forward? What do they care about and why?

4. What can you do to speed up your ability to build the right political "wiring" in the organization? Are there resources available to help you do this?

5. How can you assure that expectations are in alignment with your boss? Your peers? Your direct reports? Other importance constituencies? Could the five-conversations framework help you do this?

6. Are there other processes or resources in your new organization that could help speed up the onboarding process?

5 The International Move Challenge [*]

OSCAR BARROW KNEW HE'D EVENTUALLY END UP IN CHINA. [*] He'd spent the past ten years working his way up the ladder at U.S.–based Genera Pharmaceuticals. His ascent had been rapid— from an entry-level position in manufacturing to a general manager post in one of the company's biggest domestic plants. The next logical step was overseas experience, and Genera boasted multiple operations in China. Oscar had eagerly anticipated the challenge of managing new people in a different culture. But the ambitious executive severely underestimated how stressful the transition to an international assignment would be—for him and for his family.

Oscar had been looking for jobs outside the New York area for a while. He'd been freed up to do so after his wife, Jennifer, a partner

---

[*] This chapter was written jointly with Mark Clouse.

at a leading New York City law firm, had resigned her post to devote more time to raising the couple's two children—a newborn and a toddler.

In less than six months, Oscar secured an exciting position as the new general manager at one of Genera's manufacturing facilities in an industrial zone near Beijing. Jennifer expressed some concerns about moving to a country with such a different culture, but Oscar carefully presented his arguments: exposure to a different culture would be great for the whole family, and, financially and professionally, the opportunity was too good to pass up. The plant had grown rapidly, but had experienced serious quality and cost problems in recent months. As a result of those lapses, the previous plant manager, a well-respected Chinese national, had been let go. Oscar's new boss, the head of manufacturing for the Asia-Pacific region and a seasoned hand in Asia, had made it clear during the interview process and in posthiring discussions that Oscar's mandate was to "do what was necessary to quickly fix the plant's problems."

Oscar moved to China eight weeks ahead of Jennifer and the children, staying at an apartment near the plant. Getting away from the family gave him the time he needed to really dig into what was going on in the business. He digested all the available data on the plant's performance and spent a lot of time on the factory floor studying operations. He also questioned the existing management team vigorously about the problems and their root causes. He came away confident that he understood what needed to be done to turn things around and was certain he could fix it in short order.

Outside the office, Oscar was also working to identify potential new homes for his family. Early on, Oscar and Jennifer had decided that if they were going to commit to living and working in China, they wanted to truly immerse themselves in the culture, so they had agreed to avoid the community in which Genera's relocation services normally settled expatriates. They opted instead to live in a neighborhood favored by senior Chinese managers. As Oscar was finalizing living arrangements in China, Jennifer was dealing with similar logistics in New York: selling the apartment and physically packing and moving the family's belongings to Beijing.

As the weeks passed, Oscar faced more and more challenges on the job. All of his new team members were Chinese, and some struggled with English. They were used to being told what to do by the boss, so it was hard for Oscar to engage them in dialogue about what needed to happen. This, of course, ran counter to Oscar's preferred work style, which stressed bottom-up involvement and empowerment. At the same time, he recognized that using a directive style of leadership, in line with the team's expectations, could also have its advantages: turning the plant around *would* require clear, top-down mandates for change.

So Oscar decided to seize the initiative. Building on his detailed analysis of the plant and its issues, he crafted a turnaround plan that included shutting down a production line, rationalizing two support groups, and laying off about 5 percent of the workforce. Privately, he concluded that some of the plant's lackluster performance could be traced back to weak work from several team members, who would eventually have to be replaced. He presented the central elements of his turnaround plan to the senior team, expecting people to fall in line. Instead, Oscar left the meeting feeling like he had fallen into quicksand. The team listened politely but said little and did less. Word came back to him through HR that the perception was that the plan was "worthy of study, but very American." He also was surprised to get an unexpected call from his new boss a few days after presenting the plan, inquiring whether everything was on track.

At roughly the same time, Jennifer and the children arrived in Beijing. Now Oscar was trying to balance the job—and his frustrations with the slow pace of change at the plant—with the difficulties of transitioning the family into a new culture. Few of their new neighbors spoke English fluently. Jennifer had difficulty identifying child-care providers who had the requisite language skills. This left her isolated at home with the children, trying to set up the house and figure out the basics of living in China, including dealing with uncomfortable levels of air pollution.

Feeling alone and missing her friends and family in New York, Jennifer became increasingly despondent. Just six weeks after his family had arrived in the country, Oscar came home to find his tough corporate-lawyer spouse having a complete meltdown. Through her tears she said, "Six months ago, I was telling top executives what to do. Now the biggest decision I make is whether to bake one or two batches of cookies!"

The International Move Challenge

As more companies pursue globalization, more and more executives are leaving the comforts of their native customs and cultures to pursue leadership opportunities in other parts of the world. The stakes are high, as many companies face mature domestic markets and are counting on international expansion to drive profitable growth. Even as they seek to build strong bases of local management in strategically important countries, they need a cadre of global leaders who can manage the enterprise as a whole. But executives who can move fluidly among diverse markets and cultures are a scarce commodity. Aside from the usual questions of how to transition quickly into new roles and create the momentum for change in new workplaces, executives taking on international assignments have a couple of added pressures: settling their families into new and perhaps exotic locales, and communicating effectively with colleagues and subordinates in different cultural contexts.

Perhaps the hardest part about making an international transition is managing expectations—those of your boss, your direct reports, your family, and, not the least, yourself. There is an inescapable psychological dynamic at play when you make an international move. It's a sort of "hero's journey" that initially starts with lots of excitement and anxiety about taking charge and making a difference, along with some resentment about having to leave behind familiar people and routines. That's followed a few months later by a period of significant gloom, as the hard realities of living and working within new contexts set in. Here's where it's most important to recognize that virtually every executive who makes an international move experiences these "dark nights," and virtually everyone comes out the other side all the stronger for the experience, having built new relationships, routines, and capabilities.

As Oscar's story suggests, leaders who lack experience in making international moves can fall into common traps that can severely stress their families, negatively affect their performance at work, damage their businesses, and even lead to outright career derailment. But through my studies of international moves like Oscar's, I have identified six fundamental principles that can make the difference between a successful leadership transition and a failed one:

1. Get the family settled first.

2. Make the most of your arrival.

3. Make sure you are in compliance.

4. Build the team by building the business.

5. Take a fast first cut at strategic priorities.

6. Don't be a tourist.

Get the Family Settled First

You can't be effective in your new role if your family is struggling. It's crucial to have in-depth conversations about an international assignment with your spouse—long before you make specific decisions about which opportunities you are (and are not) willing to pursue. You'll both need to consider and discuss all the dimensions of change: the magnitude of the culture shift, the distance from "home," the type of living situation you'll be in, and, if applicable, the types of schools your children will attend. Particularly if it's your first international move, you'll need to limit the overall intensity of the change. For Oscar and Jennifer, the move to China was an enormous leap on many dimensions. Jennifer's reaction was prima facie evidence that they didn't take enough time to look at the combined impact of change on so many dimensions.

Once you've carefully considered the opportunity along these dimensions and decided to make the move, there are ways you can minimize the disruption for the family and thereby increase the odds that everyone will thrive in the new setting. If you have children, try to time the move to coincide with a natural breakpoint in their schooling. You should also arrange for extra support—from family or paid help—for your spouse during the period when you are spending significant time away from the family. This in-between time can be very stressful for everyone, especially for your spouse, who is left trying to hold things together while you head off to start an exciting new assignment. Remember, it's no fun to be stuck at home while the "hero" heads off on an adventure.

Then you'll need to focus on rebuilding family support networks as quickly as possible. If possible, identify resources (spousal support networks and advice services for expatriates) that can help at your new location *before you make the move.* Try to build some connections before you arrive, perhaps even establishing e-mail relationships so that from day one, members of your family know people in the new country. If you have children, you might try to identify other expats with children who are the same age or attending the same school. At the same time, you'll want to maintain connections to friends and family back home—regularly sending updates on the move, inviting them to visit, perhaps even establishing a Web page that recounts your family's adventures in your new home.

Oscar and Jennifer compounded their difficulties by choosing not to live with other expats in a community already set up to meet their needs. The impulse to live "with the people" is laudable but highly inadvisable when the culture change is significant and when you've never relocated to another country. A crucial factor in making a smooth transition is to retain as much of the familiar as possible. So don't just put everything into storage: if you can recreate the decor of critical family rooms in the new house or apartment—placing familiar pictures, pieces of furniture, and other personal items in bedrooms and the kitchen—it helps give family members a sense of control.

Finally, recognize that hard times for the whole family are ahead. It may take a year to reach a new point of comfort; it may take longer. But have faith that you will get there. And when everything and everyone's in doubt, go home for a visit if you want. A plane ticket is far less costly than ending an assignment prematurely.

Make the Most of Your Arrival

An actor walks onto a stage and takes his mark. Even before he opens his mouth, the audience has already come to some conclusions about what he's about to do or say. The same holds true for the executive walking into the office on the first day, first week, first month of an international assignment. It's all too easy to create the impression that you've been sent from the home office to be the conquering hero who fixes all the problems. (This is especially the case if your new role has been billed to you as a turnaround, as it was to Oscar Barrow.)

Suffice it to say, the way you "arrive" in an international assignment matters a lot. Does the manner of your arrival encourage people to share information with you, or shut them down? Does it help build your personal credibility, or undermine it? Your early actions will lay the foundation—positive or negative—for how all subsequent moves will be interpreted.

There is a natural tendency for new leaders to focus on the problems first—fix what's wrong. But this approach can be problematic when you're accepting a leadership role in a new land. You risk sending the message that you believe "there is no good here" to people who may already have a defensive mind-set about an outsider coming in; and it will take only a little reinforcement to cast "the boss's negative impression" in concrete. While this dynamic can arise in any transition situation, the potential for it to cause problems is often amplified by the anxieties new leaders face in taking their first international assignments, specifically the desire to prove they can add value. Even in the worst business environments, finding some good to build on will lift your team and give them some confidence to deal with the real issues.

To avoid this trap, you should start by asking questions, not making statements—even if you're pretty sure you know what the central issues are. Let the members of the organization validate (or disprove) your theories. Don't worry about setting up your office; go to the front lines right away, wherever they are. Talk to salespeople and others in the field, and really listen. If you start doing this on day one, the word will quickly spread across the organization. People want to believe in their leaders, and seeing them up close makes a material difference. A memo will never take the place of a conversation.

While you're still planning for your arrival, you may want to take stock of the stereotypes you might be associated with based on, say, your national culture or your history with the company. If people coming from the home office are perceived as being "too far removed" from the realities of working in developing country environments, or arrogant in their long-distance prescriptions for what international operations should do, you'll need to counter that perception. It can be powerful to play against these stereotypes—using the local language, say, or demonstrating in meetings and memos that you have taken the time to try to understand the history and strengths of the organization. Such small gestures can go a long way toward convincing people you're there to work *with* them, not simply to highlight their weaknesses and make quick fixes. In the process, you can change the perceptions not just of you and your leadership style but also of the corporate center.

Finally, take the time to develop a written plan for your entry into the company. (For guidelines on how to do this, see the box "Preparing to Enter a New Country.") Share it with your new direct reports, regional HR staffers, and your boss so they'll understand where you're coming from and how you intend to lead change at the organization. Doing so can help facilitate buy-in from these critical groups and dramatically accelerate your ability to learn about the situation and identify the critical changes you'll need to make. Additionally, this written commitment will

Preparing to Enter a New Country

Before Entry

- *Read internal and external perspectives* on the market and consumers. You won't become an expert, but that's OK; awareness is what you're after.

- *Identify local consultants* who can brief you on the state of the market and the competitive environment.

- *Learn the language*—it's not about fluency; it's about respect.

- *Develop some hypotheses* about the business situation you are entering.

  - Use the STARS model to talk with your new boss and other stakeholders about the situation.

  - Assess the leadership team—is it functioning well, and does it comprise a good mix of new and veteran, or local and expatriate, talent?

help you and your people stay focused when there are challenges or setbacks. Call it the power of the paper.

Make Sure You Are in Compliance

Business standards and the "rules of the game" can change dramatically when you move from one corporate climate to another—which is why it's critical for transitioning international executives to consider, identify, and manage compliance issues. This is especially important for leaders who are responsible for sales and operations; the risk factors here might include questionable deal-making

- Assess the overall organization using any available corporate performance and talent-pool data.

- If possible, talk to some team members to gather their insights and test some of your early hypotheses.

After Entry

Your first day, first week, and first month are absolutely critical. Without the following four-phase plan, you risk getting drawn into fighting fires rather than proactively leading change.

- *Diagnose* the situation and align the leadership team around some early priorities.

- *Establish* strategic direction and align the organization around it.

- *Repair* critical processes and strive for execution consistency.

- *Develop* local leadership talent to lay the foundation for your eventual exit.

---

practices (in sales) and poor quality control or contaminated raw materials (in operations). Such missteps can easily set your transition back months or more; instead of being focused on growth, you end up playing defense 24-7.

You can't assume that just because you've communicated your standards, perhaps through mandated training videos or workshops, everyone will automatically comply. Local perspectives on what's appropriate for business (and what isn't) won't necessarily match yours or those of the home office. Indeed, some behaviors considered illegal under the U.S. Foreign Corrupt Practices Act may actually be customary, if questionable, in your new environment.

Local auditing and other compliance systems may not fully protect you.

To avoid compliance calamities, *you have to take on the unofficial role of chief compliance officer.* You and other members of the senior team must ask those people on the front lines detailed questions about operations—"How exactly did you persuade a customer or distributor to act in that way?" or "How exactly have you managed to hit your sales target, on the nose, every month for the past three quarters?"—and keep asking them until you're all confident that business is being conducted the right way, as you've defined it. If something looks too good to be true, it probably is.

As you settle into a new role in a new country, you'll need to recognize that an appropriate amount of personal focus on compliance is critical for building a culture of good decisions—and that all initiatives in this regard must start at the top. People need to know that you and your team believe in certain standards of quality and ethics and abide by those standards in visible ways. From day one, you should talk explicitly about the importance of meeting social, ethical, and corporate standards in your meetings with critical stakeholders in the company—and keep doing so for a while. You should make a point of working with your direct reports individually, preparing them to ask the right questions of others in their quest to ensure compliance up and down through work teams and units. You may also want to create mechanisms through which people in the company can safely, perhaps anonymously, report problems or ask questions.

When potentially unethical situations arise—and they will, sooner than you think—you must be decisive and consistent. "Zero tolerance" should be your guiding mantra. If you start making compromises early, you'll find yourself on a very slippery slope. Early during Oscar's tenure, for instance, local Chinese officials asked him to endorse a visa application for a group of politicians from the local community that was planning to travel to the United States. Thinking he was building valuable relationships, Oscar signed on the dotted line, without understanding that some of the officials had been linked to corruption or that the trip should have been vetted through corporate headquarters. His acquiescence triggered several negative outcomes. First, he was viewed by officials as someone who would "play ball"— perhaps opening himself and his organization to a flood of requests. Second, and potentially more damaging, Oscar lost credibility with his own people, many of whom felt that their new leader's talk about compliance was just that. He soon realized his mistake and the delegation turned out to be relatively innocuous. He was much more careful after that, identifying wise local counsel he could rely on to help vet compliance issues, questions, and requests.

You'll need to move fast once you've identified problems. Oscar was impressed, for example, when the GM of the China business to whom he reported terminated one of the top sales representatives for unethical conduct just two weeks after learning there was an issue. There will always be some excuse: "Our rivals do the exact same thing—how else can we keep up?" or "I wouldn't have hit my numbers otherwise." But there can be no flexibility in this area. Additionally, sharing information about the misdeeds and their consequences can send a clear message about your own conviction to do things the right way.

Build the Team by Building the Business

Oscar's first instinct going into the China business was to focus on assessing the existing team and deciding who should stay and who should go. A perfectly reasonable approach, to be sure; after all, the benefits and desirability of having a team of great people to lean on are indisputable.

But the way executives in international assignments go about building their teams often has to be very different from the norm, for two main reasons. First, it can simply take longer for the transitioning manager to figure out who's really good and who isn't. Remember, employees' behavior is likely to be shaped by a wide range of local factors that can take some time for the new leader to figure out—among them, domestic-market dynamics, previous leadership, and cultural norms in the company and country. And so, six months into his new assignment, Oscar was grateful that he hadn't acted on his initial negative assessments of two key people. Both eventually proved to be highly capable leaders, but had been holding back in the early days of Oscar's tenure, feeling out the new GM before sharing their ideas and energy in full.

And second, in some international markets, where institutional infrastructures are still weak, it can be that much harder to quickly find suitable replacements for critical senior positions. So instead of using aggressive assessments as a jumping-off point, you're better off taking a more measured approach: when you factor in the time and cost of finding replacements, is it better to purge, develop, or simply stand pat with the talent you have? The obvious exception to this approach is when a team member engages in unethical behavior, or refuses to comply with the new direction in which the team is headed.

Leaders who are adjusting to vastly different cultural and organizational contexts are particularly vulnerable during those first few days and months. In some cases, because of their own insecurities, transitioning executives may shine an unnecessarily harsh spotlight on their team members' perceived shortcomings; Oscar came close to falling into this trap. In order to justify their own presence or prove to their superiors that they are serious and capable, they go into problem-finding mode. It's as much an ego-protection exercise as a diagnostic one.

But even if the new leader's intentions are good, his single-minded focus on early assessments can create a defensive environment, one in which team members can turn on one another in their struggle to stay on the island. This mind-set can ripple through the organization; alliances form, and people spend more time trying to influence personnel decisions than managing the business—all of which can make success in your new role that much more difficult to achieve.

A better way for new managers to build a team is to focus everyone on *a series of short-range goals* designed to begin to build the business. Not only does this approach provide an early rallying point for the group, but it also gives the leader invaluable feedback about team members: how they respond to this management approach will speak volumes about their capabilities. As you do this, though, be careful about raising expectations too high. The truth is, you'll almost certainly want to make some changes to the team. So it doesn't make sense to encourage deep bonds until you are reasonably confident that the core group is in place. At that point, your team-building efforts will have much more meaning, hopefully heartened by some early wins for the group to celebrate.

Take a Fast First Cut at Strategic Priorities

Leaders in their first international assignments often are shocked to find out how little information they have on which to base critical judgments about the performance and directions of their businesses. Accustomed to relying on rock-solid market and operational data, and overwhelmed by the complex and unfamiliar dynamics of a new business in a new market, it's all too easy for these executives to end up in the "foreign freeze." They become overly fixated on wringing insights out of data that just aren't there, or setting up entirely new information systems, rather than focusing on the information at their disposal and what it *really* suggests about strategic priorities.

Transitioning leaders need to recognize that operations in developing countries (owned by companies based in developed nations) can be highly fragmented, and that solid operational and market data can be hard to come by. Often these businesses were built through a series of acquisitions that were assimilated but never fully integrated, resulting in businesses that are struggling with competing priorities. Although this fortunately was not a problem for Oscar, it's not unusual for these businesses to churn through a series of leaders in a short period of time, especially if the operation is being used as a training ground for high-potential home-company executives. Most important, performance metrics (and systems of measurement) may be absent or weak.

But rather than freeze your focus on the data that's missing, you should begin to shape direction and priorities based on the information you have, taking a reasonable first cut at defining your strategic priorities and drafting plans to execute on them, while simultaneously determining ways to get the information you're missing. Better to develop some reasonable direction than no direction at all.

Without the usual base of data, this can be a challenging assignment—but it can be done, if you pay attention to four critical factors. First, make the most of the high-level information you do have. What do the numbers say about your business? Which parts of the organization are doing well, and which aren't? Which products and services are making money, and which aren't? Competitive intelligence may also be limited, but you should still be able to figure out who's winning in your market or adjacent ones, who's losing, and which of your rivals' business models and best practices might be worth emulating.

Second, develop some hypotheses about the key drivers of your business. In particular, identify *today's base* (the businesses that are contributing the most currently) and *tomorrow's potential* (the businesses that promise to contribute heavily in the future). Using this information, you can begin to draft a strategic plan that focuses on securing the base, capturing high-potential opportunities, and, perhaps most important, halting business activities that don't fall into either of these categories.

Third, based on your first-cut conclusions about strategic priorities, identify a few ways to achieve early wins and build momentum. This might include devoting a critical mass of resources to a small set of high-leverage initiatives—for instance, Oscar might have focused on figuring out how to make some rapid improvements in quality. Or it might mean killing those business activities that don't create value or whose model proves unsustainable.

Finally, you can use the information you collect during this first-cut prioritization and planning process to sketch out an early road map. The map will give you focus, help you understand how to deploy resources and talent most efficiently, and accurately underscore areas of need—for instance, where it is most important to address knowledge gaps. (Indeed, this stage is where it makes more sense to consider whether and how to build whole new information systems.) As you gain traction with your first-cut efforts, you'll need to follow up aggressively, of course, with a comprehensive, data-driven, strategic-planning process. But these initial actions are critical for creating and communicating the longer-range vision that the whole organization will get behind.

Don't Be a Tourist

You think you're an executive tackling a challenging professional assignment. But for the longtime staffers in the organization you're joining, you're a short-timer, there just long enough to be able to include the phrase "international experience" on your resume or in your development profile. And the staffers know that what the manager-as-tourist cares about most is not having anything bad happen on his watch, so they become very effective at telling the boss what he wants to hear. They keep their heads down and find ways to delay and defer taking difficult actions, figuring there's a good chance that this leader, too, shall pass.

In fact, some leaders do behave like tourists—learning the basics about the organization but not taking the time to immerse themselves deeper in the corporate and national culture, and therefore missing out on important insights and signals from employees, customers, and consumers. This is a huge mistake. Good decision making from the top and productive collaboration across the organization both flow from the leader's ability to assess and adjust to the environment.

This is not to say, however, that you should fully assimilate at the expense of what has made you an effective leader in other contexts. You'll need to strike the right balance between acculturating yourself and seeking to change subordinates' behaviors that stand in the way of achieving high performance. It's all too easy for people to use "cultural differences" as an excuse for inaction or poor performance.

Recognize, too, that understanding a culture involves much more then figuring out whether to kiss, bow, or shake hands.[1] The surface differences in customs are important, of course, but the real challenge is to understand the deeper assumptions that underpin every organization and every society—for instance, who legitimately wields power, or which groups or activities create the most value. These insights won't just help you tailor your leadership style; they are often imperative for making good decisions about how to build brands or position products or services.

So how can you speed up your ability to understand and operate in a new culture? Beyond the obvious value of reading good cultural overviews, it is definitely worth acquiring a working knowledge of the local language. It will not only differentiate you from "tourists" but may also give you unexpected insights: the structure of languages is very much a reflection of the cultures in which they developed.

Additionally, be sure to identify some "cultural interpreters"—inside and outside the company. These are people who understand both your culture and the local culture, and can help you bridge the two worlds. Ideally, you will find at least two—an expatriate who has a lot of experience working in the culture you're moving to, and a native who has a lot of experience working with expatriates. They can help you translate your intent in context-appropriate ways.

Oscar Barrow got an object lesson in the perils of cross-culture management a month into his transition when he decided to recognize the outstanding work a plant analyst had done in creating a new production-forecasting model. Oscar made a point of lauding her contribution in a meeting of all the plant supervisory staff. The reaction surprised him. Everyone looked down while the analyst squirmed uncomfortably in her seat. Only later, in a conversation with his head of HR, did Oscar realize that his public acknowledgment of one person's work ran counter to traditional Chinese culture, which emphasizes collective achievements over individual ones.

Oscar's intentions were good; he had wanted to recognize excellence as a way of encouraging others in his organization to pursue it. But he needed to reward high performance in ways that made sense within the culture. He could have framed his acknowledgments differently—perhaps offering praise and gratitude to the analyst one-on-one, but then recognizing the whole team in a public forum and taking a moment during that meeting to thank the analyst for her terrific leadership of the group.

International moves are among the most exciting transitions that leaders undertake. The personal and organizational challenges are many. But with the right mind-set, planning, and execution, these assignments can substantially stretch your capabilities and assumptions.

International Move Checklist

1. What are the major dimensions of change for your family? Is everyone really prepared for this magnitude of change?

2. What would help speed up the process of establishing the family in a new location? Can you time the move to make it less disruptive? Are there ways of beginning to build a new support network before you move? What can you do to preserve the familiar?

3. How will you approach the arrival process? What elements need to be included in your written entry plan? How will you introduce yourself to the organization? How will you spend your first week?

4. What can you do to identify potential compliance problems as early as possible? Are there potential trusted advisors you can identify *before* you move?

5. How will you approach the process of assessing the team and the business? Can you use a shared diagnostic process to accelerate your team assessment?

6. Are you prepared to commit to a minimum amount of time in the new role? If so, might it make sense to communicate this commitment to your team and the organization?

6 The Turnaround Challenge

"GET IN THERE AND STOP THE BLEEDING," DEBRA SILVERMAN was told. "Then you can figure out where we should take this business." As the newly appointed general manager of InovaMed's FemHealth business unit, Debra knew this was going to be a challenge. FemHealth had been launched three years earlier but had failed to gain much traction with its physician customers or to justify the substantial investments the parent company had made in the venture—and unacceptable losses were mounting. As a result, Debra's predecessor, who had been the driving force behind the creation of FemHealth, had been let go. Now it was Debra's job to clean up the mess.

Ohio-based InovaMed developed and manufactured medical devices and was organized into three divisions: cardiology, orthopedics, and surgical care. The latter group developed instruments and supplies for most common surgeries—sutures, scalpels, retractors, and the like. The surgical care division was the leader in its field, with strong market positions in most major product categories. Still, it was competing in relatively mature markets, and leaders in the division were aggressively scouting for potential areas of growth.

It was in this environment that Debra's predecessor had presented a compelling idea for a new business unit, which would be part of surgical care, dedicated to supporting the office-based treatment of women's health problems. The market was growing rapidly: there had been a worldwide rise in the population of women aged forty-five to fifty-five. And technological advancements had yielded minimally invasive approaches and procedures in health care that were eliminating the need for long hospital stays and costly inpatient care. In response to these trends, the number of health care facilities dedicated to outpatient care for women had risen, both in the United States and in some European countries.

As outlined in the business case drawn up by Debra's predecessor, the FemHealth unit would supply surgical devices and other products needed for the office-based treatment of women's health problems, focusing primarily on five categories of disease, including fertility, pelvic pain, and incontinence. Because these ailments were typically treated by obstetricians and gynecologists, FemHealth could then market a range of its products to these same customers, thereby achieving synergies through marketing, sales, and product servicing. The business plan had also called for the cross-pollination of products between the United States and the European Union. There was already a strong market in the United States, for instance, for the instruments used in less-invasive treatment of abnormal uterine bleeding, but not so much in Europe. Conversely, there was high demand for the instruments used to treat incontinence in Europe but less so in the United States. FemHealth planned to build on existing successes to create demand for technologies and products in other places.

The products and technologies involved in treating the target FemHealth conditions were not part of InovaMed's core expertise. So the parent company entered into a series of acquisitions and licensing agreements to build FemHealth's operations and R&D capabilities. The surgical care division was responsible for managing those functions, freeing up Debra's predecessor to focus on marketing and sales. The senior team had also decided that most of FemHealth's important support functions—including finance, HR, IT, and regulatory affairs—would be provided through shared-services agreements. As a result, the general manager of FemHealth had just five direct reports—two marketing directors, a sales director, an R&D liaison, and a person dedicated to setting up the ventures through which InovaMed marketed products outside the United States and the European Union.

Three years in, the business was in deep trouble. It had missed revenue targets for four straight quarters—partly because of poor forecasting but also because of unexpectedly intense competitive pressures in all five of the product/disease categories FemHealth had targeted. To counter this, many new-product-development initiatives had been launched, but most were behind schedule and over budget. FemHealth had also been buffeted by a product recall for an instrument to treat abnormal uterine bleeding, resulting in unfavorable scrutiny from regulators and the press. And it was struggling to make the cross-pollination strategy work; regulatory approvals of European products in the United States were proceeding much more slowly than anticipated. As a result of these setbacks, the staff was seriously demoralized.

Debra's new boss, William Butler, had given Debra's predecessor more time than was typical to fix the problems. He was used to dealing with larger, successful businesses, and he understood that it often took time for start-ups to reach critical mass. But when no obvious progress was being made, William had little choice but to fire the GM and hire someone who could turn things around.

William knew Debra well; she had a history of dealing effectively—some would say ruthlessly—with troubled businesses. Debra had started her career in R&D in surgical care's wound care business, before switching to various managerial roles in sales and then marketing. After a successful stint as a marketing VP in InovaMed's endoscopic instruments business, Debra had made the leap to country management—most recently leading a three-year turnaround of the company's struggling business in Portugal. While the business challenges at FemHealth were broader in scope than in any of her previous assignments, the promotion greatly appealed to her: It was just the sort of "fixer-upper" she relished taking on.

The Turnaround Challenge

It's essential that new leaders figure out the organizational-change challenge they're facing (using the STARS model) and then tailor their personal approaches for making the necessary changes happen. In this chapter and the next two, I will explore what this means in depth, focusing on turnarounds in this chapter, realignments in chapter 7, and diverse collections of STARS situations in chapter 8.

Debra Silverman is clearly facing a turnaround situation at FemHealth. The organization is in crisis, and there is indisputable evidence (in the form of ongoing losses) that recent attempts to improve things just aren't working. The staff is demoralized and has lost confidence in existing leadership. There's a definite sense of urgency: no thoughtful person is going to argue that Debra should proceed incrementally. The faster she can figure out what's going on, the quicker she can initiate corrective actions.

When it comes to turnarounds, speed is of the essence. That's because a turnaround is a lot like the car whose engine is on fire: you immediately pull over and extinguish the flames. Then you take the car to the repair shop, rip out the motor, and replace it with a new one. In the business context, your initial actions as the new leader of a turnaround should be just as urgent: you immediately try to stabilize the business, preserving the "defendable core" so it will survive. Then you can shift your attention toward reworking the business, laying the foundation for growth.

Business Systems Analysis

First stabilize, then transform—that should be your mantra as the leader of a turnaround situation. You'll need to quickly diagnose the situation and then define the central organizational-change challenges. To accelerate the diagnostic process, it helps to have a view of the business as a *dynamic system* comprising interdependent elements that can also be analyzed individually. (See figure 6-1.) Specifically, you'll need to focus your attention on these four important components of your organization's business system:[1]

1. *External environment:* The competitive and political challenges the business faces, as well as the expectations of important outside stakeholders.

2. *Internal environment:* The organization's climate and work culture.

3. *Business strategy:* The mission, vision, goals, metrics, and incentives that provide overall direction for the business.

4. *Business architecture:* The leadership team, skill sets, and core processes that are needed to realize the strategy.

FIGURE 6-1

The Business System Model

This graphic represents the key elements of a typical business unit. It highlights the discrete components that can be analyzed as well as the linkages among these elements. In general it is not possible to change one element of a business system without having an impact on others.

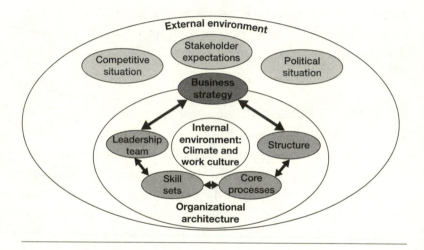

The first two can help you define the threats and opportunities your business faces; the second pair are the critical levers you can use to influence organizational performance. But these are interdependent elements, after all, so the business strategy helps to connect shareholders and other external parties to the organization. And the business architecture—aside from supporting the strategy—strongly influences the organization's climate and work culture. Let's take a closer look at each component—and at how Debra Silverman might tackle her turnaround challenge at FemHealth using the Business Systems Analysis framework.

The External Environment

At the time Debra took over FemHealth, the business was subject to intense pressures from competitors in each of the five major product/disease categories the company was targeting. It was also confronting strong political headwinds with its attempts to gain regulatory approvals for the launch and reimbursement of FemHealth products in the United States and Europe. Moreover, Debra's room to maneuver was shaped by the expectations of outside stakeholders, including her boss and the senior team at InovaMed. A detailed overview of the FemHealth scenario, based on Debra's initial diagnosis, is summarized in the box "Assessing the External Environment."

The Internal Environment

As defined earlier, the internal environment encompasses climate and work culture. The organizational climate refers to how people feel about the business and their relationship to it. The work culture refers to the ways that people in an organization communicate, think, and act—*patterns mostly grounded in their shared assumptions, values, and experiences*. When these patterns are functional, they can result in high-level performance: people hit their targets, and then some. When these patterns are dysfunctional, they can sink morale and employee engagement. At FemHealth, for instance, some managers complained about the lack of accountability at the organization, as well as prevailing issues with conflict management—both significant areas of cultural concern for Debra. A detailed overview of the FemHealth scenario, based on Debra's initial diagnosis, is summarized in the box "Assessing the Internal Environment."

Assessing the External Environment

Competitive Situation

What are the central forces shaping the competitive situation?

- The market for less-invasive treatments for common women's health problems is growing, but some segments and geographies are much more attractive than others.

- Each of the five major product/disease categories has aggressive but different and specialized competitors; the overall intensity of competition is increasing.

- The business was built on the assumption that there would be synergies—customers, opinion leaders, and technologies—among the various product categories. In reality, these synergies haven't materialized. Are they really there?

Political Situation

What are the central forces shaping the political and regulatory situations?

- Debra's predecessor and other members of the leadership team made assumptions about FemHealth's ability to transfer

The Business Strategy

If, like Debra, you are charged with turning around a business, the right place to start is usually with a cold, hard look at the business strategy: the very fact that a complete corporate makeover is required is prima facie evidence that the existing successful products from Europe to the U.S. market and vice versa. There have been issues in gaining reimbursement for these products, however. FemHealth's new-product launch plans need to be more in sync with its reimbursement strategy and discussions. The unit's plans for launching products in Asia should also be reviewed, given the potential barriers to gaining reimbursement and patient acceptance there.

- Critical government regulators in the United States have lost confidence in the business because of a recent product recall and an incident in which a patient nearly died during a procedure at which a FemCare representative was observing.

Stakeholder Expectations

What is the new leader expected to achieve and by when?

- William Butler is expecting Debra to turn things around: he wants her to stabilize the business, achieve positive cash flow within six to nine months, and reach double-digit growth in revenues and earnings within two years.

- Leaders in important support functions such as finance and HR expect Debra to come in and clean house—including replacing most or all of her new direct reports.

---

strategy is inadequate. However, few aspects of business are more fraught with complexity than strategy creation and execution.

Experienced leaders intuitively understand the need to craft powerful, coherent road maps for their organizations—but surprisingly few can articulate what strategy is and what differentiates a good one from a bad one. Moreover, as leadership teams struggle

Assessing the Internal Environment

Organizational Climate

What are the central challenges concerning climate and employee engagement?

- The team has been immersed in a vicious cycle in which it committed to a plan and then failed to meet its objectives. As a result, morale is poor across the entire organization, engagement levels are extremely low, and there is widespread cynicism among employees in lower levels of the company about the capabilities of the leadership team. Few are optimistic that the unit can turn things around, even with a new general manager.

- There are major conflicts between individuals in sales and marketing. The people in marketing believe their colleagues in sales haven't put adequate energy into executing their plans, and they've had issues figuring out incentives. For their part, the people in sales are feeling scapegoated, arguing that marketing has failed to provide sufficient focus and resources on core products.

Work Culture

What are the central challenges concerning work culture?

- When people fail to execute on their commitments, they make excuses rather than accept responsibility—probably a reflection of the organization's short but less-than-successful history.

- When mistakes are made or problems arise, there is more finger-pointing and infighting than root-cause analysis and conflict resolution—particularly between the people in sales and marketing.

to assess existing strategies and develop new ones, it's all too easy for them to get mired in semantics: Are we talking about mission, or vision? Are we really debating strategic options, or just talking tactics? Should we devise a strategy for the business as a whole, or for specific functions such as marketing or R&D?

When it comes to *defining* good strategies, certain things are clear: They create value for customers and capture value for investors over the long term. They are powerful simplifications that, when communicated effectively, provide clarity, focus, and alignment across the organization. They leverage and enhance the organization's core competencies. They respond to challenges and create opportunities in the external environment. And they are robust and adaptive, not brittle.

When the discussion turns to crafting good strategies, however, things get a little fuzzy. Is crafting a strategy the same as designing a business model? Should the strategy help determine how leaders achieve support for change and alignment throughout the organization? Does a good strategy also focus attention on how the business will learn and adapt to changing conditions? The answer to all three questions is yes. But leaders are seldom clear about which of these strategic conversations they're actually having.

To succeed in your turnaround efforts, you'll need to understand all three of the discrete dimensions involved with crafting a good business strategy. The central elements of this 3-D Business Strategy model, illustrated in figure 6-2, are as follows:[2]

1. *Designing (or redesigning) a business model* that profitably exploits specific opportunities in the external environment and that can withstand related threats.

2. *Driving organizational alignment* to ensure that employees at all levels of the organization are motivated to make decisions that are consistent with the business model and that will help the company achieve its goals.

FIGURE 6-2

3-D Business Strategy

This diagram illustrates the key elements of business strategy.

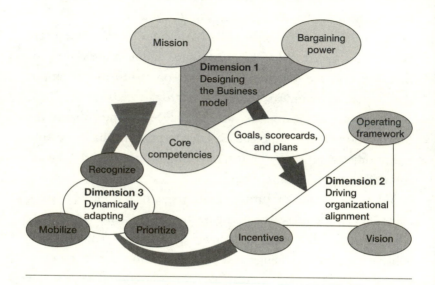

3. *Dynamically adapting* to changes in the external environment as well as proactively "shaping the game" through innovation and creative efforts to influence the political/regulatory environment.

Let's take a closer look at each of these critical dimensions of strategy.

Dimension 1: Designing (or Redesigning) the Business Model

The business model defines the core logic of the business—the rationale under which it will generate revenues, manage costs, and achieve profitable, long-term growth. Critical elements of the business model include:

- *A definition of the mission.* What is the overarching focus of the business? What will the business do (and not do) in terms of target customers, product and service offerings, and value propositions?

- *A true understanding of the business's sustainable sources of bargaining power.* How will the organization develop and sustain its ability to capture value in its dealings with customers and suppliers? How will it go about protecting its interests in interactions with policy makers, regulators, NGOs, and other nonbusiness actors?

- *A comprehensive inventory of core capabilities.* In what areas must the business excel in order to support the chosen mission and sustain key sources of bargaining power? Which tasks or processes does the business handle well internally, and which should it purchase or outsource?

These elements of the business model generally reinforce one another: a clear mission definition translates into accurate decisions about which investments to make in which core capabilities—all of which supports the central focus of the organization. Likewise, making the right investments in core capabilities can help the business to develop robust sources of bargaining power—for example, economies of scale, strong brands, and protectable intellectual property.

Indeed, as part of business-model redevelopment, it's imperative for transitioning leaders to start off by clarifying the mission—understanding that it's a stepping-stone toward refocusing the organization in the long term. This can be an important early win for new leaders: clarity about the mission begets clarity about the sources of bargaining power and core capabilities. This, in turn, facilitates the development of the second and third dimensions of business strategy: driving organizational alignment and dynamically adopting to environmental shifts.

To clarify the mission and redesign the business model, you and your senior team should ask yourselves a series of guiding questions: Which customers will we serve (and not serve)? Which products and services will we offer (and not offer)? With whom will we compete (and not compete)? What value propositions will we offer (and not offer)? And, finally, what kind of trade-offs will we need to make, and what are the implications of making those compromises? These questions impose a sort of discipline on the group and can immunize the business against "mission creep," or trying to be all things to all people. If there's a lack of strategic focus within the business, the negative effects will almost inevitably spill over to other components of the business system—as a result, the business may be hobbled in the external environment which, unsurprisingly, can contribute to a poor climate and work culture inside the organization.

To successfully turn things around at FemHealth, Debra must start by asking some hard questions about the mission and the business model. Since the company's inception, *everything* has been a priority—which means *nothing* has been. In particular, the business has been focused on too many disease categories to get sufficient focus. Without a central focus, FemHealth's leadership team hasn't been able to make the hard resource-allocation decisions necessary to establish a center of gravity for the venture. And because there is a lack of synergies among the organization's product/disease categories—that is, they don't involve selling to the same customers or leveraging the same technologies— FemHealth hasn't been able to leverage its portfolio of surgical instruments and devices to build up bargaining power with customers and suppliers. Put simply, there hasn't been a clearly articulated rationale for why the various parts of the business belong together.

Debra needs to refocus the business on two or three product/disease categories, selecting a mix that both generates cash and demonstrates significant growth potential. This product mix should also reflect real, not imagined or hoped-for, synergies—common customers, marketing channels, technology platforms, and the like. The rest of the product probably should be divested. If FemHealth lacks critical mass in its chosen product/disease categories, then Debra might want to consider additional targeted acquisitions or licensing deals.

The business model provides the basis for articulating the strategic goals, or A-list priorities, for the business. This involves being realistic about the state of the business and asking yourself: Among all the key performance indicators—revenues, costs, cash flow, and so on—which are the most critical targets to hit? And which metrics will we use to gauge our progress in achieving these top objectives?

For each critical process or quality indicator, you'll then want to establish your means of tracking performance. Structured methodologies such as the Kaplan/Norton Balanced Scorecard can be a great resource in this regard.[3] Indeed, it often helps to create a graphical representation of performance—for instance, a dashboard using conventional green-yellow-red color codes to highlight process or performance improvements, stagnation, or failures. These compact visual aids can make it easy to both communicate the A-list priorities to the organization and monitor the team's march toward achieving these goals.

Moreover, cascading high-level goals in this way inevitably triggers additional thinking from employees about focus and priorities: Given the overall revenue goal, what should the contribution of each product be? Given the overall cost-reduction goal, which areas should we target for cutting? And so on.

Finally, the scorecards and dashboards can also help generate explicit discussions about any fundamental trade-offs that need to be made in the business—for instance, "If we do *X*, we'll have to do *Y*, and we should acknowledge that up front." These discussions should obviously be informed by and consistent with the decisions the team made about the business model: what the customer value proposition is and which core capabilities the company needs to excel in. These conversations should also be baked into the organization's operating goals, as I discuss in the next section.

Dimension 2: Driving Organizational Alignment

You've redesigned the business model and defined goals and scorecards. The second step in the strategy-development process is to ensure that people throughout the organization behave in ways that are consistent with and support the model and the goals. As shown in the 3-D Business Strategy model, there are three primary levers for creating such alignment: a comprehensive operating framework, a well-considered incentive system, and a strong vision.

How do people throughout the business know how to make the right decisions? The *operating framework* provides detailed guidance for what employees *should* do in order to support the business model and the achievement of critical goals. It establishes the "wiring" by defining who gets to make which decisions and provides guiding principles for how those decisions should be made. It encompasses your business's standard operating procedures, key business rhythms, project management protocols, and crisis management routines. It also includes associated disciplines such as your organization's planning and budgeting systems. Whether it is explicitly written down or just a set of tacit understandings, the operating framework is the shared "playbook" that provides people with guidance on how to coordinate their actions.

Given that they know *how* to make the right decisions, *why* should they do so? The *incentive system* provides a core rationale for why people should want to act in productive ways. It obviously should include an appropriate mix of fixed and performance-based bonuses, individual and group rewards, and monetary and nonmonetary perks. Critically, however, the chosen mix should be directly correlated to the business's defined goals and metrics and the behaviors necessary for hitting those targets.

Finally, it's no accident that, within the 3-D Business Strategy model, *vision* and mission sit at opposite ends: they truly are the beginning and end of a business strategy. The two are often confused, but it's actually quite easy to distinguish them. Mission is about overarching goals and what will be achieved. When leaders proclaim, "We will take that hill," it's a mission statement. By contrast, *a vision gives people a reason to go the extra mile.* It is a compelling picture of a desirable future that people are inspired to realize—as when leaders declare that, "by taking that hill, we will make the world safer for your children and grandchildren." Indeed, the presence (or absence) of "inspirational" language can provide a convenient acid test for distinguishing between mission and vision.

Dimension 3: Dynamically Adapting

The third and final dimension of the 3-D Business Strategy framework is *dynamically adapting to shifts in the external environment.*

As the old saw puts it, "plans never survive first contact with the enemy." This does not mean that planning isn't important; it's critical. What it does mean is that a good business strategy must be robust in the face of shifts in the environment. Critically, it means that a sound strategy must *enable the organization to rapidly identify and respond to environmental shifts.*

The point of departure for doing this is identifying emerging threats and opportunities, establishing priorities for responding to those threats and opportunities, and mobilizing to respond. Collectively these make up the business's RPM (recognize-prioritize-mobilize) process, illustrated in figure 6-3. Related questions leaders like Debra should ask concern *how* (and how fast in comparison to competition) the business identifies shifts in the environment. Is the business being predictably surprised? What mix of

FIGURE 6-3

The RPM Process

This diagram illustrates the cyclical process that businesses must put in place to recognize emerging threats and opportunities, establish priorities, and mobilize to respond.

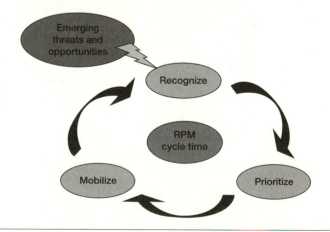

centralized and distributed intelligence-gathering mechanisms are in place? How are the information process and priorities established? And what happens once a decision is made to respond?

The Organizational Architecture

Suppose, like Debra, you're at the helm of a turnaround, you've labored to assess the external and internal environments, and you've survived the Herculean task of picking apart and redefining a failing strategy. To realize your plans for organizational change, however, you'll need to focus on another piece of the business system: the organizational architecture, or the right foundation of resources, organized in productive ways. It comprises the following four elements:

1. *The business's leadership team:* Your direct and indirect reports, who collectively are responsible for setting direction, embodying important values and behaviors, executing plans, and getting results.

2. *The business's skill sets:* The types of skills and abilities, below the senior level, required to do the work of the organization and create desired results.

3. *The business's organizational structure:* The way employees are divided into units and functions, with associated decision-making rights, and the mechanisms for achieving integration across those silos (for example, project teams and liaison roles).

4. *The business's core processes:* The way information and materials flow through the organization to convert inputs to desired outputs.

FemHealth had issues in all of these architectural areas, including problems with the quality of the leadership team, concerns about the structure of the sales and marketing organization, and weaknesses in the new-product-development process. A detailed overview of the FemHealth organizational architecture, based on Debra's initial diagnosis, is summarized in figure 6-4.

FIGURE 6-4

Assessing the organizational architecture at FemHealth

Leadership team

- The existing team is demoralized, divided, and not respected by the rest of the organization; most, if not all, of the team will have to be replaced.

- The organization needs new talent at all levels; how deep do the changes need to be?

- The business needs dedicated resources (direct reports) in critical functions such as finance, HR, R&D, operations, and regulatory affairs. Depending on the types of licensing and acquisition decisions Debra Silverman makes, additional talent may be required in those functions.

Organizational structure

- It doesn't make sense to have two marketing directors, as FemHealth currently does. The duplication only contributes to the lack of focus within marketing and perpetuates the deep rifts between members of the sales and marketing groups.

- It doesn't make sense to continue utilizing shared services, as FemHealth currently does. The large number of indirect reports and the lack of dedicated resources have created a lack of focus within the business unit—and having functions like finance and regulatory affairs operating on the periphery will make it all the more difficult for Debra to turn things around.

- FemHealth's operations (the structure and central processes, in particular) are in need of an overhaul: because that functional area was assembled through acquisitions and licensing deals, it comprises a large number of facilities with insufficient scale to be efficient. This is contributing to both cost and quality issues.

Skill sets

- There are pockets of good talent in the organization, below the level of Debra's direct reports—especially in sales. It's not clear, however, that anyone in that functional area is ready to step up and lead.

- Because critical functions operate through a shared-service structure, there is an opportunity to draw on stronger talent in these areas. In particular, Debra might seek commitments to dedicate specific talented people in critical functions such as HR, finance, and operations to her business.

FIGURE 6-4   **(continued)**

Processes

- FemHealth's demand-forecasting and business-planning processes are weak, which has contributed to the business's inability to define and commit to realistic plans.

- The R&D group's project management process is weak: too many products in development, and not enough focus. The group has also shown an inability to kill projects early when it becomes clear they lack promise. A more disciplined stage-gate process overseen by a cross-functional team might yield significant improvements.

While each of these elements of the organizational architecture can be analyzed independently, they must all fit within a coherent system: to execute the business strategy, the company needs the right leadership team, the right levels of talent placed in the right work groups, and efficient processes that produce the right outputs.

Therefore, an important piece of diagnostic work turnaround leaders like Debra Silverman must do early on is to assess whether misalignments among elements of the architecture are hobbling the business. Is FemHealth failing because the strategy is inadequate, or because the organization lacks the talent to implement the strategy properly? (As the details in the figure suggest, FemHealth's existing strategy is deeply flawed.) Does the way FemHealth has organized people into work teams makes sense given the company's goals? (The short answer is no—the shared-service structure ends up diffusing FemHealth's overall focus and hinders its ability to leverage strong talents within and outside the company.)

Turnaround Checklist

1. What are the key challenges in the external environment? What issues with customers and competitors have become particularly damaging to the business? Do the

business's problems flow in part from regulatory, political, or social issues?

2. What is the existing business strategy? Why has it failed? Is it because the business model was inadequate? Because alignment was not driven down through the organization? Because the business was unable to adapt as quickly as its best competitors to shifts in the environment?

3. How might the business be better focused? What should it do and not do? What are the sustainable sources of bargaining power? At what must the business excel?

4. Is the operating framework adequate to align actions and decisions? Are incentives aligned with the business model and key goals? Is there a compelling vision of a desirable future?

5. How effective is the business at recognizing emerging threats and opportunities? At establishing priorities for responding? At mobilizing rapidly? How might the RPM process be accelerated?

6. What are the strengths and weaknesses of the existing architecture? What changes need to be made in the leadership team? In key skill sets? In the structure? In core processes?

7 The Realignment Challenge

IF STEFAN EISENBERG KNEW ANYTHING, IT WAS HOW TO manage in times of crisis. After all, he'd overseen a relatively quick and successful turnaround of European manufacturing operations at Careco Devices, a multinational medical devices company. He was less sure, however, that this sort of approach would be effective in his new role at the firm.

Before joining Careco, Stefan, a hard-driving, no-nonsense executive, had spent fourteen years moving up the ranks in manufacturing at a leading automaker headquartered in southern Germany—starting as a productivity analyst and ending up as the general manager of the firm's largest assembly plant. Senior-level slots at the car company were in short supply, and Stefan didn't want to work for a competitor, so he decided to take his world-class operations management expertise to a new company in a new industry.

After a series of interviews and a period of negotiation, Stefan joined Careco Devices as a senior vice president of manufacturing operations. The company was based in the United States but had operations in more than fifty countries and a long history in Europe. It boasted a regional structure, with distinct organizations in North America; South America; Europe, the Middle East, and Africa (EMEA); and Asia-Pacific. This was primarily because the company often needed to gain market-specific approvals for new products and certification of manufacturing processes. Stefan and his family relocated from southern Germany to Zurich, Switzerland, headquarters for Careco's EMEA organization.

Stefan had originally been brought into Careco with a mandate: turn around manufacturing operations in Europe. He had moved decisively to restructure an organization that was broken because of the company's overemphasis on growth through acquisition and its focus on country-level operations to the exclusion of other opportunities. Within a year, Stefan had centralized the most important manufacturing support functions, closed four of the least-efficient plants, shifted a big chunk of production to Eastern Europe, and reduced overall head count by almost 15 percent. These changes, painful though they were, began to bear fruit by the end of eighteen months, and operational efficiency continued to improve: three years after the changes had been rolled out, the company's facilities were in the top 20 percent of benchmarked plants in Europe.

But no good deed goes unpunished: Stefan's success in Europe led to his appointment as executive vice president of supply chain for Careco's core North American operations, headquartered in New Jersey. The job was much bigger, combining manufacturing with strategic sourcing, outbound logistics, and customer service. With his appointment, the previously separate divisions were united in a single, end-to-end supply chain.

In contrast to the situation in Europe, Careco's North American operations were not in immediate crisis—which Stefan began to realize was the essence of the problem. The long-successful organization had only recently shown signs of slipping. The previous year, industry benchmarks had placed the company's manufacturing performance slightly below average in terms of overall efficiency and in the lower third in the crucial area of customer satisfaction with on-time delivery. Mediocre scores, to be sure, but nothing that screamed "turnaround." In addition, the sorts of structural problems that had given Stefan low-hanging fruit to pick in Europe weren't present in North American operations. For instance, there was already an appropriate balance of centralized and decentralized manufacturing support functions in the plants.

Stefan's own assessment of the group, however, indicated that serious trouble was brewing. First, a close look at operations revealed a disturbing pattern of minor failures all along the supply chain—in planning, supplier integration, forecasting, and plant reliability. Initiatives had fallen between the silos, and when mistakes were made, there was more finger-pointing than troubleshooting going on—telltale signs of tension, even hostility, among units that had previously been stand-alone operations. Stefan believed there were better ways to integrate the four major pieces of the supply chain for which he was responsible.

Second, he noted the U.S. managers' penchant for reveling in their ability to respond to full-blown crises rather than avoid problems in the first place. Problems would come up, but the so-called solutions the executives came up with merely addressed surface symptoms rather than root causes—which of course ensured that similar problems would reemerge in the future. The leaders who were most respected in this "culture of heroism" were those who vaulted into action, swords in hand, ready to charge into the breach. It had become clear to all that the organization highly valued individuals' crisis-mode capabilities. As a result, people had learned to perpetuate and thrive on chaos.

Third, Stefan also felt that the executives relied too much on intuition, rather than impartial information, when making critical decisions, and that the North American organization's information systems provided too little of the right kind of objective data. These shortcomings contributed, in Stefan's view, to widespread and largely unfounded optimism about the organization's future. This, in turn, fueled more firefighting: because executives reflexively viewed the glass as half full, they consistently failed to respond to early signs of trouble. They acted only when problems became large and undeniable.

Finally, Stefan recognized early on that he was saddled with various constraints to improving operational efficiency. For instance, the CEO of Careco Devices had publicly stated that the company would refrain from exporting U.S. jobs—either directly through plant construction or indirectly through outsourcing—to lower-wage nations for the next three years. As a result, none of the existing plants was an obvious candidate for closure; and while there were a few obvious opportunities for streamlining supply chain operations and reducing headcount, the resulting efficiency gains would be very modest.

Factoring in all this early information, Stefan concluded that North America's performance problems had more to do with its culture than its strategy, structure, or systems. There was a strong commitment to teamwork and a lot of pride in what the organization had accomplished. But, particularly in manufacturing, there was just too much firefighting going on. Given what he'd accomplished in Europe, Stefan knew that people were expecting him to come into North American operations wielding a very big knife. But the transitioning executive wasn't sure he wanted—or needed—to play according to that script.

The Realignment Challenge

Stefan's story illustrates a common dilemma facing leaders who make inter- or intracompany moves: the importance of assessing and understanding the type of business situation they are inheriting. Specific to Stefan's move to North American operations, is he facing a turnaround similar to the one he managed in Europe or a realignment scenario? Indeed, it will be nearly impossible for him to come up with an effective strategy for creating and supporting organizational change, and succeed in his new role, if he can't recognize the important underlying differences between these two business situations—which can look remarkably similar on the surface.

The central difference is "sense of urgency." As I noted in chapter 6, a turnaround situation is a lot like the car whose engine is on fire—the problem is obvious, and the driver's response must be immediate and dramatic. That was the situation Stefan faced in Europe; urgent needs required urgent actions from him and his team. By contrast, a realignment situation is like the vehicle whose tires are slowly but inexorably losing air—the problem easily goes unnoticed over time, and the driver usually responds only after one or several wheels have gone flat. This is the scenario Stefan is facing in North America: the business problems are emerging slowly—so gradually, in fact, that they aren't setting off many (or any) alarms.

Each transition scenario obviously demands very different change strategies from the new leader. In turnaround situations, for instance, the first priority for the transitioning executive is stabilization: restore some sense of equilibrium to the organization, its people, and its operations. Once that's been achieved, the next steps are to preserve the remaining "defendable core" of the business—taking radical actions if necessary—and to identify opportunities for growth. But in realignments, the first order of business is education: the new leader must create a sense of urgency among people, many of whom won't even recognize there is a problem. (See figure 7-1.)

As I discussed in chapter 6, the typical approach to change in turnarounds involves retooling the organization's architecture, focusing first on strategy and structure and then on processes and skills; then creating a new, high-performance culture; and, finally, shifting employees' attitudes from despair to hope. This is essentially what Stefan did in Europe. He closed plants, shifted production, and cut the workforce dramatically (a strategy shift). He also rapidly centralized important manufacturing functions in order to reduce fragmentation and cut costs (a structural shift).

Unfortunately, if Stefan tries to adopt a similar change strategy in Careco's North American manufacturing operations, he could easily trigger the firm's organizational immune system, prompting his boss, peers, and direct reports to summarily reject him and his ideas. (For more on organizational immunology, see chapter 4, "The Onboarding Challenge.")

Particularly in an environment in which many people are in denial about the need for change, premature efforts to alter the organization's strategy or tinker with its structure may be viewed as superficial or unnecessary—and will have a hard time gaining support. Consider that North American manufacturing operations aren't experiencing any major capacity or productivity problems, so plant closures aren't necessary (no need to change strategy). Critical manufacturing functions are already centralized and strong (no need to change structure). The real problems are in the quality of the company's information systems and its somewhat pyromaniac culture—dynamics typical in many realignment situations. Indeed, organizational performance in North America may be showing signs of decline in part because previous leaders were prone to changing strategies and structures before dealing with other issues first.

FIGURE 7-1

Turnaround change versus realignment change

Fundamental principles	Turnarounds	Realignments
1. Organize to learn Figure out what you most need to learn, from whom, and how you can best learn it.	Focus on technical learning (strategy, markets, technologies, and so on). Prepare to act quickly.	Focus on cultural and political learning. Prepare to act deliberately.
2. Define strategic intent Develop and communicate a compelling vision for what the organization will become. Outline a clear strategy for achieving that vision.	Prune noncore businesses.	Hone and leverage existing capabilities. Stimulate innovation.
3. Establish A-item priorities Identify a few vital goals and pursue them relentlessly. Think about what you need to have accomplished by the end of year one in the new position.	Make faster, bolder moves. Focus on strategy and structure.	Make slower, more deliberate moves. Focus on systems, skills, and culture.
4. Build the leadership team Evaluate the team you inherited. Move deftly to make the necessary changes; find the optimal balance between bringing in outside talent and elevating high potentials within the organization.	Clean house at the top. Recruit external talent.	Make a few important changes. Promote high potentials from within.
5. Secure early wins Think through how you plan to "arrive" in the new organization. Find ways to build personal credibility and energize the ranks.	Shift the organizational mind-set from despair to hope.	Shift the organizational mind-set from denial to awareness.
6. Create supporting alliances Identify how the organization really works and who has influence. Create key coalitions in support of your initiatives.	Gain support from bosses and other stakeholders to invest the required resources.	Build alliances sideways and down to ensure better execution.

Your decisions about which fundamental elements of the organization to tackle first, and which approach to use, are just the beginning, of course. In a realignment versus turnaround scenario, you'll also have to define and secure early wins differently—the most important one being raising people's awareness of the need for change—and you'll need to handle personnel issues quite differently. For instance, to expeditiously turn around the European business, Stefan had to clean house at the top of the organization and bring in new senior talent from outside the organization. In North America, however, the leadership team he has inherited is reasonably strong—perhaps offering the transitioning leader a good case for promoting from within.

The Right Change Strategy for the Situation

Once you're clear about the type of business situation you've inherited—turnaround or realignment—you can define the strategies you'll employ to create the necessary changes in the organization. In realignment scenarios, it will be critical for you to mount a nuanced transformation effort—much more patient and subtle than the direct, dramatic actions that Stefan took in Europe and that were required in the turnaround situation described in chapter 6. The focus here has to be on, first, progressively raising awareness of problems; and, second, changing the attitudes and behaviors of a critical mass of people in the organization.

Raising Awareness

You'll need to pierce through the denial and get everyone in the organization focused on preventing emerging problems from becoming much more serious. The following principles can help you alter the collective consciousness.

Emphasize facts over opinions. You can change the shade of your company's culture from rose-colored to black and white simply by putting more emphasis on fact-based management and root-cause analysis. For instance, in Stefan's early operational review meetings in North America, he and his team drilled down into issues where opinions were not backed up by facts. In those sessions, Stefan didn't punish people for not having all the answers to his questions; instead, he firmly required that they go out and do some research to support or disprove their statements. *His mantra was not "bring me answers, not problems"—a dangerous philosophy that can give team members a handy excuse for not raising tough issues.* Rather, Stefan preached informed intervention: "Bring up issues early, and come prepared to talk about how you'll diagnose root causes and begin to deal with them."

Shift the focus outward. In realignments, it's common for organizations to have become inwardly focused—relying solely on internal process performance benchmarks. To counter this, you'll want to start bringing the outside world in, as much as possible. That might mean engaging in explicit benchmarking within your industry or even across industries. Stefan introduced explicit external benchmarking into the conversation at Careco's North American manufacturing operations. He commissioned studies comparing the company's manufacturing numbers and customer satisfaction scores with those across the industry. The studies revealed his organization was in the bottom quartile, which provided a big wake-up call.

Recruit others to help educate your people. As a new leader, you obviously need to force the people in the company or unit you're joining to confront reality, but it's always dangerous to be the sole source of pain in a group—you run the risk of becoming the main target for an attack from the organization's immune system. One way to avoid this is to bring in outside voices—customers, suppliers, or even respected leaders from other parts of the business—to help say the things some people might not want to hear. Stefan greatly enhanced his efforts to raise organizational awareness about slack performance by bringing in impartial assessments from respected business consultants, drawing on expert voices from outside the company to help make his case.

Elevate the champions. More so than firms in need of a turnaround, companies requiring some sort of realignment typically still have a fairly strong pool of executive talent. So a powerful way to send a message to employees about the need for change is to elevate those people who exemplify the type of thinking you believe is necessary to lead the organization into the future. For instance, Stefan knew he'd have to make a few high-payoff changes within his team. Specifically, a few of the central positions in manufacturing required leaders with strong technical skills to support the systems changes he planned to make. Instead of looking outside for that expertise, however, Stefan promoted from within. People came to see that he wasn't just focusing on the weaknesses of the business; he was also appreciative of its strengths.

Remove the blockers. *Sometimes there is no substitute for the ritual sacrifice of an implacable opponent.* In Stefan's case, there was an influential manager in the North American supply chain operations who, despite Stefan's best efforts, didn't grasp the need for change; in fact, the manager's inaction threatened to undermine Stefan's plans and attempts to establish his leadership. That person's departure sent a very important message to the rest of the organization.

Changing Attitudes and Behaviors

Research on human motivation has shown that the relationship between people's attitudes and their behaviors is complex and bidirectional.[1] Changes in attitudes do lead to persistent changes in behavior—but the reverse also is true, and often the effect is greater. That is, if you can get people to act differently, it will lead them to think differently. Research suggests that people are uncomfortable when there's a mismatch between their actions and their beliefs, so they inevitably correct for it, aligning what they think with what they do. Therefore, it's critical for new leaders in realignment situations to focus initially on altering behaviors, understanding that attitudes will change over time. The following principles can help.

Engage people in shared diagnosis. If you gather people to work on a problem, they go in with certain assumptions—namely, that there *is* a problem. If you gather people to generally explore or diagnose a business situation, they don't feel forced to reach conclusions about possible solutions, or about the depth of transformation needed, until they are prepared to so do. I call this an "entanglement strategy."[2] You move people from point A to point B in a set of digestible steps rather than in a single leap. Stefan did this by setting up teams to focus on specific elements of performance across the supply chain rather than discrete "problem" areas. To lead the teams, he appointed people from each of the four operations segments whom he knew to be influential but who didn't necessarily agree with him. As a result attention was focused on key handoffs between silos.

Change the metrics. People evaluate their performance according to a company's or unit's established metrics—for instance, number of products sold, amount of revenues earned, or number of satisfied customers. If you change those measures, you'll inevitably change people's behaviors (hence influencing their attitudes). The important point to note here, however, is that any change in metrics must be viewed by the team as necessary and legitimate. For instance, Stefan created a new, compact set of core metrics at Careco, shifting the emphasis from lagging indicators to leading ones. In this way, he was able to focus his team's attention on overall supply-chain performance, rather than discrete, functional outcomes. And by shifting the group's attention toward predictors of future problems, he ultimately affected how team members allocated their time.

Align incentives. *If you reward people (through recognition, status, and advancement) for fighting fires, you shouldn't be surprised if you end up with an organization of pyromaniacs.* To get people more interested in preventing predictable surprises, Stefan had to get them moving in the same direction—providing positive incentives for avoiding fires and less-positive incentives for fighting them. This basic principle also extends to dealing with conflicts between units in your organization. You could easily attribute these tensions to mutual mistrust between groups or differences in personality. Most of these conflicts, however, are the result of differing incentives. To increase the peace among the supply chain units, and to reduce finger-pointing among team members, Stefan established "team incentives" directly linked to the new set of supply-chain metrics he had introduced. Initially, team members complained about being held accountable for others' mistakes. Over time, however, they started helping one another. As their behaviors changed, so did their attitudes about the new setup of the supply-chain organization.

Build bridges from the past to the future. In realignment situations, where things haven't completely broken down yet, it makes sense to build on the organization's strengths in order to fix its weaknesses. This means building bridges (from where people are to where they need to be) rather than just jettisoning people and ideas. To kick-start the transformation process, for example, Stefan convened Careco's top 150 supply chain managers in a series of sessions in which they collectively examined the company's core systems, skills, and culture. They were challenged to identify strengths that could be leveraged and weaknesses that should be addressed. Among the cultural strengths the participants identified were deeply held values around both teamwork and responsiveness. The corresponding cultural weaknesses were tendencies to ignore problems until they became very serious and to engage in too much firefighting. Armed with this insight, Stefan and the managers were able to have progressive discussions about how to preserve the productive elements of the culture while uprooting the dysfunctional ones.

Secure and celebrate early wins. When you're trying to change behaviors and attitudes in a realignment situation, it's critical to achieve momentum—generating movement in promising directions and leveraging small gains to accomplish still more. So the instant you achieve some significant, measurable progress, you should declare (interim) victory and celebrate. This provides both visible acknowledgment that early efforts are beginning to bear fruit and an opportunity to recognize specific individual and team efforts that exemplify "right thinking."

The Right Leadership Style for the Situation

The state your organization is in influences not just how you lead change efforts but also how you manage yourself—specifically, how you adapt your personal leadership style to the situation and build a team of people who complement your strengths and compensate for your weaknesses in the new context. This is particularly true when it comes to figuring out whether you are reflexively a "hero" or a "steward."[3]

Heroes and Stewards

In organizational turnarounds, leaders are often dealing with people who are hungry for hope, vision, and direction—which necessitates a heroic style of leadership, charging against the enemy, sword in hand. People line up behind the hero in times of trouble and take direction. Clearly, this was the case for Stefan in Europe. A heroic leader by nature, he immediately took charge, set a course, and made some very painful calls. Because the outlook was bleak, people in the business were willing to act on his directives without offering much resistance.

Organizational realignments, by contrast, demand something from leaders more akin to stewardship—a more diplomatic and less ego-driven approach that entails building consensus around the need for change. Stewards are more patient and systematic than heroes in deciding which people, processes, and other resources to preserve and which to discard.

Accomplished heroes and stewards share many important attributes: they are typically grounded in basic values that people admire, such as a strong work ethic and a sense of fair play. Both types of leaders are perceived as committed to solving their organizations' problems. They challenge others (and themselves) to achieve the highest possible performance. They clearly communicate what needs to be done, forge connections with the people who work with them, and courageously pursue needed change. (See the graphic summary in figure 7-2.)

FIGURE 7-2

Heroes and stewards

This graphic illustrates both the common elements of effective leadership and key elements that differ depending on the situation.

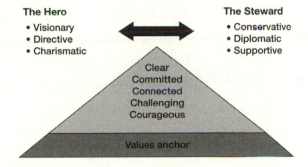

But, *depending on context*, heroes and stewards also need to exhibit fundamental differences in their approaches to leading change. What if Stefan approached his new role in North America as "Stefan the Knife," and tried to set a new direction and make painful changes using the same heroic strategies that made him successful in Europe? Chances are great that his ideas (and even the man himself) would be rebuffed, particularly because he's coming from the outside: a foreign organism that triggers a powerful reaction from the organization's immune system. The result could be disabling, or even fatal, to his ambitions. So the natural hero must, when confronted with a realignment situation, tap into his inner steward. In his North American appointment, for instance, Stefan needed to make careful assessments of the situation, move more deliberately toward change, and lay the foundations for sustainable success.

Conversely, leaders who are more naturally stewards can struggle in turnaround situations. People in crisis are hungry for hope and direction, not necessarily for involvement and consensus. The situation usually calls for quick action, not systematic deliberations and discussions about shared visions and support. So the natural steward must, when confronted with a turnaround situation, tap into her inner hero—critically, while still preserving the basic management skills and approaches that have made her so effective as a leader.

Building Complementary Teams

While you'll need to adapt elements of your leadership style to the business situation you face in your role, you obviously can't be something you're not. There are, after all, limits to leadership alchemy; and whether you are a hero or a steward, you won't easily be able to tear down and then rebuild the foundations of your personal leadership style.

What you can adjust, at least to some degree, are particular aspects of your basic leadership approach. For instance, how do you learn in new situations? In the European turnaround situation, Stefan needed to rapidly assess the organization's technical dimensions—its strategy, competitors, products, markets, and technologies—much as a consultant would. In the North American realignment situation, however, Stefan's learning challenge was markedly different. Technical comprehension was still important, obviously, but cultural and political learning mattered more. Internal dynamics are usually one of the root causes when successful organizations begin to drift toward trouble—and getting people to acknowledge the need for change is much more a political challenge than a technical one. Particularly for a newcomer to the organization, as Stefan was, a deep understanding of the culture and politics is a prerequisite for leadership success—and even survival.

Moreover, you should seek out team members whose skills and styles complement your own. If you are reflexively a hero but the situation you are in demands more stewardship, you should identify those people in the organization for whom stewardship is more of a natural role. Indeed, at the core of all great leadership teams are two or three executives who exhibit the right mix of heroism and stewardship—taking the pressure off any one to play multiple roles. The steward helps to curb the worst impulses of the hero: impulsivity, micromanagement, and, in the extreme, narcissism. Meanwhile, the hero can counteract the steward's tendencies toward risk aversion and perhaps too much consultation and consensus building.

The roles each leader will play are likely to be obvious, based on individuals' tendencies, but the mix of styles necessary will change as the business situation does. In the crisis management phase of a turnaround, for instance, there is obviously a need for directive, heroic leadership. But once things have stabilized, the senior team will want to quickly cast its focus forward, toward tasks such as building leadership capacity in the organization—the work of stewards. Likewise, once the deliberations have been held and diagnoses discussed, every realignment scenario will have initiatives and programs that will demand bold and decisive action—work that calls out for a hero (or two).

Leveraging the STARS Framework

The STARS (start-up, turnaround, accelerated growth, realignment, and sustaining success) framework discussed in the introduction should be a standard component in any company's change-management portfolio. By distinguishing among types of business situations, STARS helps leaders identify the kinds of change that are required and figure out how best to initiate the transformation process as they transition into new roles. Given the dynamism of the business environment, companies are experiencing more or less continuous change—some realignments, some turnarounds, some other flavors of transition. It behooves companies to equip new leaders with change processes and tools tailored to the different STARS situations.

The STARS model should also play a big role in how companies approach leadership assessment and team development. Simply put, firms should have a model for effective teamwork that is rooted in several realities. First, businesses are typically run by a core group of two or three people with complementary strengths. And second, the right mix of executives depends on the business situation. An important supporting plank for this is an assessment tool that gives insight into the team role preferences of leaders.

The STARS framework also can provide important insight into recruiting and onboarding challenges. External hires brought in to turn around a deeply troubled organization face quite different risks from those charged with realigning a business that is on the path to serious problems. *Care must be taken, for example, not to set new hires up for failure by placing them in realignment situations and expecting them to create a sense of urgency unaided.*

Finally, companies can incorporate the STARS framework into their talent management and succession-planning processes. Well-rounded business leaders have to be able to manage the range of STARS situations. It wouldn't pay to produce, say, only turnaround specialists or realignment leaders. Most businesses display a mix of change situations; some elements are in turnaround, some in realignment (and some in accelerated growth and sustaining success). So it can be powerful to assess high-potential leaders in terms of their experience dealing with diverse STARS situations, and to use this information to identify critical talent gaps and opportunities to fill them.

Realignment Checklist

1. Why has the organization begun to slip from sustaining success to realignment? Are key people in denial about the gathering storm? If so, why is this happening?

2. Are the root causes of the problem about inadequate strategy or structure or, more likely, are they about the systems, skill sets, and culture of the organization?

3. What aspects of the work culture support high performance and which undermine it? How have the negative aspects taken root and why have they been permitted to persist?

4. What can you do to raise awareness of the need for change? Is there key data that can help make the case? Would a shift in metrics help? Are there influential voices outside the organization, such as customers, to whom people might listen? Would some shared diagnosis help?

5. What kind of leader are you reflexively? A hero or a steward? What does the situation demand, more heroism or more stewardship?

6. Given the needed mix of heroism and stewardship, how might you build a complementary team that will help you realign the organization?

8 The STARS Portfolio Challenge

ANDY DONOVAN WAS HIRED INTO ZETACAM, A CONSUMER electronics company, as vice president of customer service. He was responsible for the company's three major regional service centers, which had just recently been consolidated; they had previously operated as independent units. An experienced operations manager, Andy understood that he was expected to improve performance in all three centers while harmonizing their structures, systems, and cultures.

In his first two weeks on the job, Andy traveled to each of the centers to meet with the regional directors and their staffs, as well as the front-line supervisors and their employees. He wanted a firsthand look at how the centers were organized, how they used resources and technology, and what their climates and work cultures were like. This information, he figured, would help him define his priorities and develop an improvement plan to present to his new boss, Zetacam CEO Christine Rau.

In his travels, Andy encountered three quite different business situations. The first center he visited gave him cause for both encouragement and concern. The good news was that it consistently provided timely, high-quality service to customers. Furthermore, his interviews with front-line supervisors and employees revealed that the center boasted strong processes and systems and, most important, a well-trained and serious-minded workforce proud of its problem-resolution capabilities and its reputation for high performance. Andy was troubled, however, by a subtle but unmistakable attitude of complacency among some center employees. When he questioned them about plans for improvement, for example, he got the sense that they didn't think there was much need or opportunity to drive things forward.

The second center was managed by the longest-serving of the three regional directors. It was also the largest of the three centers, serving customers in some of the most heavily populated areas of the United States. Andy's review revealed a history of good performance but signs of slippage in the past twelve months—the chief one being an uptick in the number of customer complaints. But when the VP interviewed the director and his team, and the supervisors and their subordinates, he was struck by their lack of concern about this issue. The site's customer satisfaction scores had dipped only slightly—and that was mostly because of product quality issues and resource constraints, the managers and employees told Andy. The customers were becoming "too demanding," they said. For his part, the regional director seemed happy to downplay the problems. He also seemed a bit burned out, Andy noted. The VP concluded that, without even recognizing it, this customer service center was, little by little, losing its effectiveness.

The third center had very serious problems—performance woes that had, in part, driven Zetacam's decision to consolidate the management of its customer service centers and hire Andy.

Customers' complaints had been piling up and were becoming increasingly strident—grievances that could be heard all the way up the organization's chain of command. In his discussions with center managers, supervisors, and employees, Andy discovered a seriously demoralized workforce. Employee turnover was unacceptably high and many of the supervisory losses were people who had been identified as having high potential. The regional director, Barry Shields, had been brought in just eight months prior, ostensibly to right the ship. He had immediately spent heavily on new information technologies that he believed were critical for boosting performance. Facing budget pressures, Barry had cut everything else down to the bone. So far, however, there was little to show for all those investments in IT. There were certainly glimmers of progress at this center, Andy thought, but he left the building convinced that this group would require lots of his attention.

Back at headquarters, Andy contemplated his strategy for improving customer service operations. He wanted to preserve the positive attributes of each center but also integrate critical structures and systems as well as eliminate the root causes of negative performance. Even during this period of transition, the centers had to maintain acceptable levels of customer support; he couldn't afford a severe drop in satisfaction scores.

Andy had no direct reports beyond the three regional center directors. He had planned to reach out to his peers in corporate HR and finance for advice and possible resources. But each of the customer service centers also had staffers in critical functions—such as operations, quality control, and training—from whom he could potentially draw ideas. After digesting his observations and jotting some notes about how to proceed, Andy sat down with his new boss. He started to share his impressions, but Christine cut to the chase: "Are you planning to replace Barry?"

The STARS Portfolio Challenge

In the previous two chapters, I outlined how new leaders should transition into specific business situations as defined by the STARS model—turnarounds in chapter 6 and realignments in chapter 7. The reality, however, is that you'll rarely encounter a "pure" situation. It's much more likely that you, like Andy Donovan, will inherit a complex mix—a STARS portfolio, with different parts of your organization immersed in their own unique business situations.

The good news is that the tools developed in the two preceding chapters can still be applied in such complex environments. You can use the systems-analysis approach outlined in chapter 6 to conduct a thorough diagnosis of the discrete business situations you're facing in various parts of the organization. And you can use many of the proactive change tools discussed in chapter 7 to develop your approach to creating and building the momentum within different business segments. The crucial difference, however, is that you'll be dealing with multiple STARS situations in parallel. This has major implications for how you should organize to create momentum, how you should build your team, and how you should adapt your leadership style to diverse pieces of the business.

First off, however, you need to get a good read on all the possible STARS situations being reflected in your organization—which means conducting a *STARS portfolio analysis*, as illustrated in figure 8-1. You can slice and dice the organization in a variety of ways—looking at units, products, projects, customers, processes, or facilities. The "right" unit of analysis will depend on the nature of your responsibilities. For instance, it definitely makes most sense for Andy to consider the customer service centers as his primary point of analysis.

FIGURE 8-1

The STARS portfolio analysis grid

At different times during your leadership tenure, different parts of your organization will almost certainly be thrust into transitional situations unique to that particular unit or function. The following grid can help you map out the various STARS situations reflected in your organization and determine your priorities for creating change.

First, select a unit of analysis (pick one).

Organizational units	☐
Customers	☑
Products	☐
Projects	☐
Processes	☐
Facilities	☐
Countries	☐

Then, use your chosen unit of analysis to assess which pieces of the organization belong in the various STARS categories.

STARS type	Unit of analysis	Priority points
Start-up		
Turnaround	Customer service center three	50
Accelerated growth		
Realignment	Customer service center two	35
Sustaining success	Customer service center one	15
	Total	100

The next step is to denote which pieces of the business belong in which STARS category—start-up, turnaround, accelerated growth, realignment, sustaining success—using the table in the figure. For instance, Andy can clearly categorize the first Zetacam service center as being in a sustaining-success scenario; the second as being in a realignment situation; and the third center as being in a turnaround state. Note that you don't necessarily have to fill up the entire table; it's entirely possible that all the pieces of your business will fall under just one or two categories.

Now do some quick-and-dirty prioritization. Using the right column, take 100 "priority points" and divide them among the units of analysis represented in your STARS portfolio, according to the time and attention you think you'll need to give each during the next six months. It's plausible, for instance, that Andy would decide to allocate 50 percent of his time to the turnaround of service center three; 35 percent of his hours to the realignment of service center two; and 15 percent to ensuring that service center one continues to sustain its success.

Finally, put an asterisk in the grid next to the type of STARS situation you most prefer managing. Some executives may relish the fast-track challenges of turning around a foundering organization; others might thrive on managing the incremental but impactful changes that can be necessary in realignments or sustaining-success situations. Marking your personal preference can help you recognize whether your priority ratings reflect the true needs of the organization or simply your own biases—the business problems you particularly enjoy tackling and the ways you like to work. If you put the asterisk next to the STARS category to which you also assigned the largest number of points, you are either tremendously fortunate that the business challenges you're facing match up so well with your preferred areas of focus, or your personal preferences have skewed your priorities.

Driving Execution

Once you've charted the mix of STARS situations reflected in your organization, you can use the information to determine the approach you should use to create momentum for change—which leads us to a discussion about the science of driving execution.

FIGURE 8-2

Organizational thermodynamics: An overview

Execution engines transform "fuel" in the form of talent, funding, and support into work—the early-win initiatives that will help to create momentum.

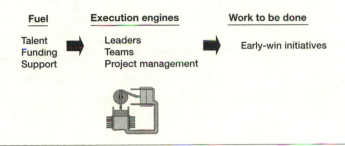

Fuel	Execution engines	Work to be done
Talent	Leaders	Early-win initiatives
Funding	Teams	
Support	Project management	

Physicists and researchers for centuries have been studying thermodynamics—the process by which engines turn fuel into motion. Similarly, transitioning leaders who are dealing with a complex mix of STARS situations must quickly become experts in something I call *organizational thermodynamics*—the means by which a business's products and processes (execution engines) convert its human and financial capital and management support (organizational fuel) into the right early wins (forward motion). As illustrated in figure 8-2, the execution engines comprise dedicated project teams, led by people who can get things done and supported by robust systems and processes.

Identifying Your Centers of Gravity

To design powerful execution engines for your organization, you must begin "with the end in mind," as the author Stephen Covey so aptly put it in *The Seven Habits of Highly Effective People*.[1] In this case, the desired goal is to secure some early wins that will help you build the momentum for change in the business. You'll need to identify three or four areas in which you have a good chance of realizing rapid improvements—think of them as your "centers of gravity." The best candidates are business problems that you can get to relatively quickly, that won't require too much money or other resources to fix, and whose solution will yield very visible operational or financial gains. Obvious targets might be those parts of the business you had categorized as being in turnaround mode in your STARS portfolio analysis grid. Andy, for instance, should think hard about how to achieve some quick improvements in customer service center three; first, though, he decided to assemble a SWAT team of high performers from the other two centers and task them with identifying priority improvements. This can't be the only center of gravity he focuses on, obviously, but it's an important start because of the extent of the problem and the magnitude of senior management concern.

In your assessments, it's important to keep the STARS states top of mind: how you go about getting early wins will obviously depend on the context. For example, because customer service center three is in a turnaround situation, Andy needs to quickly stop the bleeding. That would constitute a good early win. But in customer service center two, which is mired in a realignment situation, Andy will have to find ways to make people aware of problems they can't see at this point. The new VP will also have to confront complacent staffers in customer service center one, which is trying to sustain its success, as well as identify effective ways to transfer best practices from that center to the others.

Besides acknowledging the context, you'll want to maintain your focus: if you take on more than three or four significant initiatives, spread across the different parts of the organization, you risk diluting your efforts. *Think about it in risk-management terms:* pursue a small set of initiatives so that big gains in one area will balance any disappointments in another.

As you're identifying how and where to achieve early wins, consider two additional factors: first, don't get caught in the *low-hanging fruit trap*—focusing all your energies on achieving small tactical victories that don't contribute to the overall campaign. Yes, early wins should help you create change in the short term; but they should also help you lay the foundation for achieving longer-term goals. Second, it always pays to find out what your boss considers "early wins." For Andy Donovan, this means thinking hard about how to respond to Christine Rau's blunt question about firing the regional director of service center three. Her query is a sure sign of her concerns for that unit and a sure sign to Andy that his attention is needed there. Still, if Andy fires Barry without taking time to consider whether the director's ideas and plans are likely to bear fruit, or whether Barry has the right competencies but simply needs more support, he may send the wrong signals to others in center three. (For help identifying and assessing your potential centers of gravity, see figure 8-3.)

After a period of analysis, Andy ended up identifying four initiatives he would use to secure early wins: in addition to turning things around in customer service center three, Andy wanted to standardize performance measurement and evaluation across all three centers, share best practices from center one with the other two units, and assess the costs and benefits of centralizing several important center functions. Then he turned his attention to securing the necessary resources from corporate and organizing his team (and himself) for action.

Fueling Up

Once you've identified your targets for early wins, you'll need to muster the resources necessary to achieve them—the people, funding, and time required to execute your selected initiatives.

FIGURE 8-3

Early-wins evaluator

For each possible center of gravity, carefully answer the following questions, then total the scores. The results should serve as a rough indicator of the potential for creating quick and impactful improvements in that particular area of the business.

Potential Center of Gravity: _____

Circle the response below that you think best describes potential early wins in this center of gravity.

	Not at all	To a small extent	Somewhat	To a significant extent	To a great extent
Does this center of gravity offer an opportunity to make substantial performance improvements?	0	1	2	3	4
Can these improvements be achieved in a reasonable amount of time, using available resources?	0	1	2	3	4
Would success in this area help to lay the foundation for achieving your one-year goals?	0	1	2	3	4
Would success in this area be viewed as a significant win by your boss?	0	1	2	3	4

Total your scores, and write that number here: _____

The result will be a number between 0 and 16. You can use this rough measure to compare the attractiveness of several candidate focal points. Obviously, the higher the number, the better. Initiatives that score higher than 12 are very good bets; those that score under 8 are marginal. Take care to use common sense in interpreting these numbers: If the candidate opportunity scores 0 on the first question, for example, it really doesn't matter if it scores 4s on all the others.

These resources constitute the fuel that will power your engines of execution.

In part, you'll fuel up, so to speak, by making important decisions about who's on your team and what the strategic direction should be (defining the mission, the objectives, the core competencies of the organization, and other critical elements of the strategy). But you'll also need to take a hard look at existing patterns of activity in the organization you're joining: how are people spending their time, and what does that say about their priorities, work habits, and individual strategies? This was, in part, what Andy was looking at in his early assessments of the three centers. The resulting insights served him well when the time came to focus energy on his early-win initiatives.

A good way to uncover these patterns is to ask the members of the team you inherited to list the top ten things they spend time doing in a typical week and the rough percentage of effort allocated to each. You'll naturally have to be cautious when interpreting the results; people won't be completely transparent in their recordings of how and where they devote their energy. But the data may reveal which activities are receiving disproportionate amounts of attention and which activities could use more. Their responses may also provide useful fodder for a "stop-alter-continue-start" analysis (see figure 8-4). In other words, to secure the early wins you've targeted, what will you stop doing to free up resources? What will you alter to better align employees' efforts with your objectives? Which tasks and processes should remain status quo? And what new patterns will you try to initiate?

Andy Donovan's review of the activity patterns in Zetacam's three customer service centers revealed which projects and processes were consuming more value than they were creating. His assessment also suggested that there was still significant duplication of efforts across the three centers, which justified the original plan to consolidate and pointed out areas of particular focus for Zetacam's

FIGURE 8-4

Stop-alter-continue-start assessment

While assessing your resources, identify which current activities you will stop, which you will alter in significant ways, which you will continue pretty much as they are, and which you will start altogether.

Stop	
Alter	
Continue	
Start	

new customer service VP. Using all this information, Andy was able to plan his projects and initiatives, and the necessary resources, for pursuing early wins.

Building Your Execution Engines

Once you have garnered the resources necessary to make change happen, it's time to construct the execution engines that will actually ensure that the work gets done. This critical stage requires much consideration; after all, *how you achieve the early wins is as important as the victories themselves.* Indeed, the approach you use to drive execution can be a powerful tool for ridding the organization of its worst dysfunctions. So your execution engines should be able to perform double duty: facilitate quick and early organizational improvements, and establish new standards of behavior.

Every early win sought should be viewed as a project to be managed; the makeup of the execution engine will naturally flow from your definitions of project charters, your assignment of the project teams responsible for those charters, and the disciplined project management methods your people employ. You'll obviously need to pick the right people to lead these projects—and not necessarily just the reflexive supporters of what you're trying to do. Sometimes putting a thoughtful skeptic in charge of an early-win project can be a powerful way to win over an important ally.

Beyond thinking hard about project leadership, you should also be disciplined about outlining the project focus—carefully defining the scope and goals—and thinking through the politics involved with project oversight and participation. It may be important, for instance, to have influential representatives from critical constituencies involved from the start so they can help build support for changes implemented as a result of the project.

Finally, you'll also need to take inventory of the skills and time commitments necessary to get projects done—and then follow up by providing resources and support. Do the project teams have the right kinds of expertise? Do the team members need additional training—more information about structured problem solving, for instance, or team-building methodologies? This inventory process provides yet another opportunity for establishing and rein-forcing new norms of behavior.

When building your execution engines, consider using the FOGLAMP project-planning template shown in figure 8-5. FOGLAMP is an acronym for **f**ocus, **o**versight, **g**oals, **l**eadership, **a**bilities, **m**eans, and **p**rocess. As the name implies, this tool can help you cut through the haze of organizational minutiae and illuminate the essentials.

STARS and the Personal Adaptive Challenge

Leaders who are dealing with a collection of STARS situations must be cognizant of not just how they manage discrete parts of their organizations but also how they manage themselves. As I

FIGURE 8-5

FOGLAMP project-planning template

Element	Plan

Focus

What is the focal point for this project? Where will you seek to get early wins?

Oversight

How will you oversee this project?

Who else should participate in order to help garner support for implementing results?

Goals

What are the goals?

What are the intermediate milestones and time frames for achieving them? Who will be responsible for the various pieces of the overall project?

Leadership

Who will lead the project?

What training, if any, do they need in order to be successful?

Abilities

What mix of skills and constituencies need to be included?

Who needs to be included because of his or her skills and knowledge?

Who needs to be included because he or she represents important constituencies?

Means

What additional resources does the team need to be successful?

Process

Are there change models or structured processes you want the team to use? If so, how will they become familiar with the approach? And how will you ensure that they employ it in a disciplined manner?

have stressed throughout the book, transitioning executives should seek to understand both the organizational-change challenges and the personal adaptive challenges associated with their new roles. When you're facing a complex mix of STARS situations, there are typically two main personal adaptive challenges: adjusting your leadership style to deal appropriately with the various pieces of the business, and building a team that complements you so you can capitalize on your strengths, compensate for your weaknesses, and channel your energies in the areas best suited to your skills and interests.

In those first few hours, days, and months in a new leadership role, you'll naturally want to look forward—toward the challenges you face, the strategies you'd like to employ, the personal and professional goals you'd like to meet. Instead, it might be more helpful to look back at your history in various STARS situations. Take a few minutes to record your experiences leading start-ups, turn-arounds, accelerated growth scenarios, realignments, and sustaining-success situations (see figure 8-6).

Are your experiences mostly concentrated in one or two STARS situations, or more broadly? How do your experiences align with the assessment of your STARS portfolio at the beginning of the chapter? That is, does the situation play to your strengths or does it focus on STARS categories with which you have less experience? Recall, too, the discussion in chapter 7 about heroes and stewards. When you're leading a complex mix of STARS situations, the issue is not whether you should focus on being one or the other; the issue is figuring out which style will be most effective in different parts of the business, and who is going to provide the right mix of heroism and stewardship.

If Andy has a heroic style of leadership, for instance, it would be natural and perhaps appropriate for him to want to focus on

FIGURE 8-6

Tracking your STARS trajectory

*Use the grid below to chart your experiences with particular STARS situations.
In the first column, identify the significant management jobs you've had in
your career. Categorize each job based on the type of STARS situation you
confronted and the experiences you gained there. Put check marks in the
appropriate cells, then tally up the number of check marks in each column.
This should give you a rough sense of your STARS experience to date.*

Jobs	Start-up	Turn-around	Accelerated growth	Realign-ment	Sustaining success	Shutdown
1.						
2.						
3.						
4.						
5.						
6.						
7.						
8.						
9.						
10.						
Total						

the turnaround in customer service center three. Likewise, it
would be appropriate for him to appoint a hero to lead the project team charged with coming up with a turnaround strategy for
that center. But a bigger challenge for him will be deciding who
will provide the necessary stewardship in centers two and one,
which are facing realignment and sustaining-success situations,
respectively. Will Andy personally be able to adjust? And, based

on his ability to alter his leadership style (or not), whom should he pick to lead the early-win projects at those sites?

Based on your self-assessment, you may also need to think about whether or how to develop yourself as a STARS generalist. There will always be a market for management specialists, of course—especially for turnaround artists. But the reality is that most management positions, and virtually all business careers, require leaders who can deal with the full spectrum of STARS situations.

Looking outward, toward your direct reports, your assessment of the team you've inherited should also reflect your understanding of the collection of STARS situations you inherited. Do you have the right talent on hand to accomplish your goals? Based on team members' experiences in certain STARS situations, whom should you assign to which roles? It's not uncommon to inherit a team that could easily handle a realignment situation—but would get eaten alive during a turnaround. Indeed, if you need to recruit or promote new talent, it's very much worth keeping the STARS portfolio concepts in mind to make better-informed hiring decisions. Before you start interviewing, take a step back and ask: which part of the STARS portfolio am I hiring this person to manage? If the skills match, the offer should be a relatively easy one to make.

STARS Portfolio Checklist

1. What is the mix of STARS situations that you have inherited? What are your priorities across the portfolio?

2. What are your STARS preferences, and how much experience do you have in the various categories?

Is there a risk that you will focus too much attention on the STARS categories that you most prefer?

3. Given the portfolio you have inherited, what are the implications for where and how you will seek early wins in the various parts of the business?

4. What are the most promising centers of gravity? Are there ways you can drive improvement across the entire business? Leverage resources in one area to get wins in another?

5. Given your early-win objectives, how will you marshal the resources to go after them? What do you need to stop doing?

6. How will you build and manage the execution engines you need to get your early wins?

Conclusion

Designing Companywide Transition-Acceleration Systems

THROUGHOUT THE BOOK I HAVE EXPLORED THE DIVERSE tough transitions that leaders face, focusing on how to match strategy to the demands of specific situations. I also have offered some advice about what companies can do to accelerate the various types of transitions.

To conclude, however, it is essential to take a step back from the diversity of transitions and return to an exploration of their underlying unity. While each of the transition types has distinct features and demands, they all confront new leaders with the same fundamental imperatives: to diagnose the situation rapidly and well, to crystallize the organizational-change and personal adaptive challenges, to craft a plan that creates momentum, and to manage them for personal excellence.

What are the implications for how companies should accelerate key transitions? First, companies should recognize that *effectiveness in transition acceleration is an essential element of enterprise risk management and a potential source of competitive advantage.* Success in reducing the rate of personal leadership failure in transitions reduces the risk of organizational failure or damaging underperformance. Also, if you can help all the leaders in your organization make faster, better transitions, it will help you to be more nimble and responsive than your competitors.

Given this, a second implication is that companies should *manage leadership-transition acceleration as they would any critical business process.* Managing transition risk means putting in place the right structures and systems to accelerate everyone. It also means having the right metrics and incentives in place to assess transition risk and rigorously evaluate the impact of transition-acceleration systems in managing it.

A third and final implication is that *it doesn't make sense to design different systems to accelerate different types of transitions.* When I see companies designing dedicated approaches to onboarding or promotion or international moves, I believe it to be a waste. Why? Because there is an underlying unity among the many distinct types of transitions. So it is both feasible and desirable for companies to design unified systems to *accelerate everyone.* Such systems consist of (1) a shared framework, (2) a set of tools and techniques that help leaders apply the framework appropriately given the type(s) of transitions they are experiencing, and (3) the right network of people playing key roles in support of the process.

By doing so, companies are able to institutionalize a common "language" for transition acceleration that everyone speaks. Leaders who learn it in one transition can apply it (with appropriate modification) in all the subsequent ones they experience. They also can appropriately support the many transitions that go on around them, as direct reports, peers, and bosses take new roles. The ultimate goal is to embed transition-acceleration thinking deep in the culture of the company.

Given this, how should companies approach designing comprehensive transition-acceleration "solutions"? In a decade of work with leading companies, I've developed a robust set of "design principles" that can be applied to build the right solution for your company.

1. Deliver transition support just-in-time

Transitions evolve through a series of predictable stages. New leaders begin their transitions with intensive diagnostic work. As they learn more and gain increasing clarity about the situation, they shift to defining strategic direction (mission, goals, strategy, and vision) for their organizations. As the intended direction becomes clearer, they are better able to make decisions about key organizational issues—structure, processes, talent, and team. In tandem with this, they can identify opportunities to secure early wins and begin to drive the process of change in their organizations.

The type of support that new leaders need therefore shifts in predictable ways as the transition process unfolds. Early on, support for diagnosis is key. Later, the focus of support should shift to defining strategic direction, laying the foundation for success, securing early wins, and so on. Critically, new leaders need to be offered transition support in digestible blocks. Once they are in their new roles, they rapidly get immersed in the flow of events and can devote only very limited time to learning, reflecting, and planning. If support is not delivered in small pieces, the new leader is unlikely to use it.

The design goal is to provide new leaders with the support they need, when they need it, throughout their transitions.

2. Leverage the time before entry

Transitions begin with selection or promotion, not when leaders formally enter their new positions. The time prior to entry is a priceless period during which new leaders can begin to learn about their organizations and plan their early days on the job. Upon formally entering their new organizations, new leaders are invariably swept up in the day-to-day demands of their offices.

Organizational transition-acceleration systems should therefore be designed to help new leaders get the maximum possible benefit during whatever preentry time is available to them. This means supporting new leaders' learning processes by providing them with key documents and tools that help them to plan their early diagnostic activities. For executives it may be beneficial to have coaches engage in preentry diagnosis and create summary reports on the situation.

The design goal is to leverage the time prior to entry to help jump-start the learning process.

3. Create action-forcing events to propel the process forward

The fundamental paradox of transition acceleration is that *leaders in transition often feel too busy to learn and plan their transitions.* While they know that they should be tapping into available resources and devoting time to planning their transitions, the urgent demands of their new roles tend to crowd out this important work.

Although it helps to leverage the time before entry and to provide just-in-time support, transition processes also need to provide "action-forcing events." These are key meetings with coaches or cohort events that bring leaders in transition into more reflective mind-sets.

The implication is that transition support should not be designed as a free-flowing process in which the leader sets the pace. It is better to create a series of focused "events"—coach meetings or cohort sessions—at critical stages. After undertaking some preentry diagnosis of the situation and helping the leader to engage in some self-assessment, for example, the coach and client are well positioned to have a highly productive "launch meeting."

When transition coaching is provided it therefore is critical that the new leader and the coach connect early on in a focused and meaningful way. This is one reason it can be beneficial for coaches to engage in intensive preentry diagnosis: they have a precious resource—knowledge about the situation—that they can convey to the new leader. Their insight, offered in the critical early phases of the transition, can help to cement the coach-client relationship.

The design goal is to create a series of action-forcing events that help to drive the transition-acceleration process forward.

4. Provide additional, focused resources to support specific types of transitions

The First 90 Days principles can usefully be applied in all transition situations. However, the way the principles are applied and the specific priorities new leaders pursue vary significantly depending on the types of transitions they are experiencing. It therefore is often helpful to identify the most important types of transitions the company needs to support, and develop specific, targeted additional resources to support them.

In particular, there often are good reasons to provide new leaders with additional resources for dealing with two common types of transitions:

- *Promotion.* As discussed in chapter 1, when leaders are promoted they typically have to alter their approach to leadership in predictable ways. The competencies required for them to be successful at the new level may be quite different from what made them successful at their previous level. They also may be expected to play different roles, exhibit different behaviors, and engage with direct reports in different ways. So focused sets of resources that help newly promoted leaders "take it to a new level" help to accelerate these transitions.

- *Onboarding.* As discussed in chapter 4, when leaders join new organizations or move between units with distinct subcultures, they face major challenges in (1) learning about new cultures, (2) building the right sorts of relationships and supportive alliances, and (3) aligning expectations. Focused, accessible resources for helping them to understand what it take to "get things done" in their new organizations can help to reduce derailment and speed time to performance. In working with one global health care client, for example, I developed a set of Harvard Business School–like case studies on the company history and culture, as well as overviews of key businesses.

This is not a full list of potential transition types. International moves, for example, are an important category for many companies. It simply provides a starting point for assessment.

The design goal is to identify the most important, distinct types of transitions to be supported and then (1) provide guidance for how the core frameworks and tools should be applied and (2) provide additional, targeted transition-support resources as appropriate.

5. Match delivery mode and extent of support to the level of the leader

If cost were not an issue, every transitioning leader would get intensive, highly personalized support. In an ideal world, a new leader would be assigned a transition coach who would undertake an independent diagnosis and brief the person on the results prior to entry. The coach would help the leader engage in self-assessment and identify key transition risk factors. The coach also would help support the diagnostic planning and goal-setting processes, assist with team assessment and alignment, gather feedback on how the leader was doing, and, of course, be available to the new leader as needed to talk through specific issues.

Because their impact on the business is so great, it may in fact make sense to provide very senior leaders with this level of transition support. But it doesn't make economic sense to provide it to leaders at the director level, even if sufficient skilled coaching resources are available.

The solution is to (1) identify alternative modes through which to deliver transition support (for example, coaching versus cohort sessions versus webinars and e-learning), (2) assess their relative costs and benefits, and (3) match delivery modes and extent of support to key levels in the company's leadership pipeline in order to maximize the return on investment (see figure C-1).

The design goal is to provide support in ways that maximize the associated ROI given the level of the leader in transition.

FIGURE C-1

Matching delivery mode to leadership pipeline level

	Transition support delivery modes
Frontline supervisor	Webinar series and workbooks or 1-day program and initial launch support
Manager of supervisors	2-day intensive workshop and initial launch support
Function leader (typically a VP)	Acceleration coaching for VPs (less intensive)
Business unit leader	Acceleration coaching for BULs (more intensive)
Group leader	Custom transition planning and coaching
C-level executive	Custom transition planning and coaching

6. Clarify roles and align the incentives of the key supporting players

Finally, for any given new leader, there typically are many people who potentially can impact the success of the transition. Key players may include bosses, peers, direct reports, HR generalists, coaches, and mentors. While primary responsibility for supporting a transition may be vested with one individual—typically a coach or HR generalist—it is important to think through the supportive roles that others could play and to identify ways to encourage them to do so.

The boss, for example, has an obvious stake in getting the new leader up to speed quickly, but also may be dealing with other pressing demands. So careful thought must be given to providing bosses and other key players with guidelines and tools that allow them to be highly focused and efficient in supporting their new direct reports. HR generalists likewise can provide invaluable support to leaders who are onboarding by helping them to navigate the new culture. But once again, they both need to know what to do and have incentives to do it.

The design goal is to get key players in the new leader's "neighborhood" to provide the right amount of the right type of transition support.

In summary, the key goals in designing transition processes are to:

- Institutionalize a common language that bosses, direct reports, and peers can use to communicate about key transition issues.

- Provide new leaders with the support they need, when they need it, throughout their transitions.

- Leverage the time prior to entry to help jump-start the diagnostic process.

- Create a series of action-forcing events that help to drive the process forward.

- Identify the most important, distinct types of transitions to be supported and then (1) provide guidance for how the core frameworks and tools should be applied and (2) provide additional, targeted transition-support resources as appropriate.

- Provide support in ways that maximize the associated ROI given the level of the leader in transition.

- Get key players in the new leader's "neighborhood" to provide the right amount of the right type of transition support.

Notes

Introduction

1. I conducted this study while at IMD, the leading European business school, in the spring of 2008. The survey was sent to 1,200 senior HR leaders who had attended programs or were otherwise affiliated with the school. There were 143 respondents for a response rate of 12 percent.

2. Michael D. Watkins, *The First 90 Days: Critical Success Strategies for New Leaders at All Levels* (Boston: Harvard Business School Press, 2003), p. 27.

3. Dan Ciampa, with whom I coauthored *Right from the Start: Taking Charge in a New Leadership Role* (Boston: Harvard Business School Press, 1999), makes the important distinction between *technical advice* (How can we best design a market research study?) and *political counsel* (Who is likely to resist my change initiative, and what can I do about it?). He also distinguishes between *internal advisors* (within the organization) and *external advisors* (a personal, portable network). See Dan Ciampa, *Taking Advice: How Leaders Get Good Counsel and Use It Wisely* (Boston: Harvard Business School Press, 2006).

4. I developed an earlier version of this model in chapter 3 of *The First 90 Days*. The original version included just four business situations—start-up, turnaround, realignment, and sustaining success. After working with the model for several years, I added a fifth situation—accelerated growth. The version presented in this book was first published in Michael Watkins, "Picking the Right Transition Strategy," *Harvard Business Review*, January 2009.

5. The leadership pipeline model was developed in R. Charan, S. Drotter, and J. Noel, *The Leadership Pipeline: How to Build the Leadership-Powered Company* (San Francisco: Jossey-Bass, 2000).

6. 3-D Business Strategy is a registered trademark of Genesis Advisers LLC.

7. One unpublished study I did, for example, showed that close to a quarter of the managers in typical *Fortune* 500 companies take new roles each year.

8. Two clients who implemented Genesis Advisers transition acceleration programs did their own studies of the impact. Leaders self-reported 30–40 percent improvements in their time to break even. ROIs for the program were estimated to be 400 percent in one and more than 1000 percent in the other.

Chapter 1

1. See chapter 1 of Michael Watkins, *The First 90 Days: Critical Success Strategies for New Leaders at All Levels* (Boston: Harvard Business School Press, 2003).

2. See B. Joseph White and Yaron Prywes, *The Nature of Leadership: Reptiles, Mammals, and the Challenge of Becoming a Great Leader* (Washington: Amacom Books, 2006).

3. Drucker developed this idea in his classic *The Effective Executive*, originally published in 1966. See Peter Drucker, *The Effective Executive: The Definitive Guide to Getting the Right Things Done*, 4th ed. (New York: Collins Business, 2006).

4. William Shakespeare, *As You Like It*, Act II, Scene VII, lines 139–166.

5. The leadership pipeline framework was developed in Ram Charan, Stephen Drotter, and James Noel, *The Leadership Pipeline: How to Build the Leadership-Powered Company* (San Francisco: Jossey-Bass, 2000). It's a good, albeit in my opinion incomplete, framework for looking at level-specific transition challenges. I decided that it merited inclusion here, along with some additions and modifications.

6. Those promotions were relatively recent for many of the respondents and perhaps were looming quite large in their minds as they answered the survey questions. But even taking a potential "recency bias" into account, I think it's fair to say that the shift from functional leader to business unit leader is a challenging transition worthy of study. Although fine work has been done by Harvard Business School's Linda Hill and others on becoming a manager for the first time, surprisingly little has been written about the experience of being promoted from functional leader to business unit leader. See Linda Hill, *Becoming a Manager: How New Managers Master the Challenges of Leadership* (Boston: Harvard Business School Press, 2003).

7. "Seven seismic shifts" is a trademark of Genesis Advisers LLC.

8. For an in-depth discussion of predictable surprises, see Max Bazerman and Michael Watkins, *Predictable Surprises: The Disasters You Should Have Seen Coming and How to Prevent Them* (Boston: Harvard Business School Press, 2004).

Chapter 2

1. See Elisabeth Kübler-Ross, *On Death and Dying* (New York: Scribner, 1966). See also a good description of the model at http://en.wikipedia.org/wiki/Kübler-Ross_model.

2. For a discussion of fair process, see W. C. Kim and R. Mauborgne, "Fair Process: Managing in the Knowledge Economy," *Harvard Business Review*, July–August 1997.

3. This process is believed to have been developed by an HR team at General Electric in the early 1970s. See Steven V. Manderscheid and Alexandre Ardichvili, "New Leader Assimilation: Pruess and Outcomes," *Leadership & Organization Development Journal* 29, no. 8 (2008): 661–677.

Chapter 3

1. Jim Sebenius and David Lax developed the idea of winning and blocking coalitions. See D. Lax and J. Sebenius, "Thinking Coalitionally," in *Negotiation Analysis*, ed. P. Young (Ann Arbor: University of Michigan Press, 1991).

2. For a discussion of sequencing and its role in alliance building, see Lax and Sebenius, "Thinking Coalitionally," and J. Sebenius, "Sequencing to Build Coalitions: With Whom Should I Talk First?" in *Wise Choices: Decisions, Games, and Negotiations*, eds. R. Zeckhauser, R. Keeney, and J. Sebenius (Boston: Harvard Business School Press, 1996).

Chapter 4

1. This result comes from the same study of 1,200 senior HR leaders with 143 respondents referenced in the introduction.

2. This is an adaptation of the work of Edgar Schein. Schein developed a framework for analyzing culture on three levels—artifacts, norms, and assumptions. Artifacts are the visible signs that differentiate one culture from another, including symbols such as national flags, anthems, and styles of dress. Norms are shared rules that guide "right behavior" (for example, concerning modes of greeting and eating) and appropriate conduct for people at different levels in the social hierarchy. Assumptions are the deeper, often unspoken, beliefs that infuse and underpin social systems. See Edgar H. Schein, *Organizational Culture and Leadership*, 2nd ed. (San Francisco: Jossey-Bass, 1992).

3. There is an extensive literature on social networks and influence. For an article intended for practitioners, see D. Krackhardt and J. R. Hanson, "Informal

Networks: The Company Behind the Chart," *Harvard Business Review*, July–August 1993): reprint 93406.

Chapter 5

1. This is a reference to the (very useful) book on business culture by Terri Morrison and Wayne Conaway, *Kiss, Bow, or Shake Hands: The Bestselling Guide to Doing Business in More Than 60 Countries*, 2nd ed. (Cincinnati: Adams Media, 2006).

Chapter 6

1. This is an organizational open systems model, of which there are many. The original was the McKinsey 7-S framework, which was developed in the 1960s. For an overview see Jeffrey Bradach, "Organizational Alignment: The 7-S Model," Harvard Business School Note 497045, 1996.

2. 3-D Business Strategy is a registered trademark of Genesis Advisers LLC.

3. See Robert S. Kaplan and David P. Norton, *The Balanced Scorecard: Translating Strategy into Action* (Boston: Harvard Business School Press, 1996), as well as the other books that followed in their series on measurement and strategy.

Chapter 7

1. See, for example, "Influencing Behavior," chapter 2 in P. Zimbardo and M. Leippe, *The Psychology of Attitude Change and Social Influence* (New York: McGraw-Hill, 1991).

2. For a discussion on this and other influence strategies, see Michael Watkins, "The Power to Persuade," Harvard Business School Note 800323, 2000.

3. This conceptualization was inspired by my exposure to the work of Richard Olivier and Nicholas Janni, the founders of Olivier Mythodrama. They do remarkable work with leadership archetypes, building on the seminal research of Joseph Campbell on the "hero's journey" as well as work in Jungian psychology.

Chapter 8

1. Stephen Covey, *The Seven Habits of Highly Effective People* (New York: Free Press, 2004).

Index

About the Author

Michael D. Watkins is the world's leading expert on accelerating transitions. He is the Chairman of Genesis Advisers (www.genesisadvisers.com), an executive on-boarding and transition-acceleration company located in Newton, Massachusetts. Previously he was a professor at IMD in Switzerland, INSEAD in France, the Harvard Business School, and the Harvard Kennedy School of Government.

Dr. Watkins is author of the international bestseller *The First 90 Days: Critical Success Strategies for New Leaders at All Levels*, which the *Economist* recognized as "the on-boarding bible." With more than 500,000 copies in print, 420,000 copies sold in English, and translations in 27 languages, *The First 90 Days* has become the enduring classic reference for leaders in transition. Recently it was named one of the best 100 business books of all time.

A prolific writer, Dr. Watkins is the author or coauthor of numerous articles and books on leadership. His most recent publications include "Picking the Right Transition Strategy" (*Harvard Business Review*, January 2009), "The Three Pillars of Executive On-boarding" (*Talent Management*, October 2008), and *Shaping the Game: The New Leader's Guide to Effective Negotiating* and *Predictable Surprises: The Disasters You Should Have Seen Coming and How to Avoid Them* (Harvard Business School Press).

A native of Canada, Dr. Watkins received a degree in electrical engineering from the University of Waterloo, did graduate work in law and business at the University of Western Ontario, and completed his PhD in decision sciences at Harvard University.

YOUR TRANSITIONS TOOLKIT—FREE ONLINE

Whether you are the CEO of a global enterprise or a first-time manager, you can take on your challenges with greater success today—using a suite of free downloadable resources provided by transitions expert Michael Watkins.

 DIAGNOSTIC TOOL
Take the Transition Risk Assessment. In just 15 minutes, you can measure your personal "risk index," and pinpoint exactly which tools and strategies can help ensure your greater success.

 VIDEO
Watch Michael Watkins address some of the challenges inherent in the "leadership crucible" of change—and recommend ways that you can prepare yourself to avoid failure while positioning yourself for still-greater things.

 CHECKLIST
Create "relationship capital" with true influencers using the author's Stakeholder Checklist. This tool can help you identify people inside and outside your organization who can help move your agenda forward.

 PODCAST
Gain even deeper insight and advice from Michael Watkins in a discussion of the key challenges you will inevitably face. Plus, hear about some best practices that you can adopt to take charge quickly and effectively in your first 90 days.

 DOWNLOAD THESE FREE TOOLS TODAY
www.YourNextMove.net